Missouri Real E

Missouri Real Estate License Exam: Best Test Prep Book to Help You Get Your License!

The Ultimate Workbook: Salesperson and Broker Exam-Passing Strategies

Table of Content

1. Introduction..3
2. Understanding the Missouri Real Estate Market......................5
3. Eligibility Criteria...9
4. Application Process..14
5. Exam Format..19
6. Property Ownership and Land Use Controls........................24
   - Mock Exam Property Ownership and Land Use Controls..........31
7. Laws of Agency and Fiduciary Duties.................................49
   - Mock Exam Laws of Agency and Fiduciary Duties..................54
8. Property Valuation and Financial Analysis...........................72
   - Mock Exam Property Valuation and Financial Analysis............76
9. Financing..93
   - Mock Exam Financing...98
10. Transfer of Property..115
    - Mock Exam Transfer of Property....................................120
11. Practice of Real Estate and Disclosures............................138
    - Mock Exam Practice of Real Estate and Disclosures.............143
12. Contracts..160
    - Mock Exam Contracts..165
13. Real Estate Calculations...183
    - Mock Exam Real Estate Calculations...............................188
14. Specialty Areas..205
    - Mock Exam Specialty Areas..209
15. Ethics and Legal Considerations.....................................226
    - Mock Exam Ethics and Legal Considerations.....................231
16. Day of the Exam...249
17. After the Exam: Next Steps...253
18. Career Development..258
19. Conclusion..263

Introduction

Hello and welcome to "Missouri Real Estate License Exam: Best Test Prep Book to Help You Get Your License!" If you've picked up this book, it's likely that you're considering a career in real estate in the state of Missouri, or perhaps you're already on that path and are looking for the best way to prepare for the state's licensing exam. Either way, you're in the right place. This book aims to be your comprehensive guide, providing you with all the information, strategies, and practice you'll need to not only pass the Missouri Real Estate License Exam but also to succeed in your future career.

Why Real Estate?

Before diving into the nitty-gritty of exam preparation and real estate principles, let's take a moment to consider why a career in real estate is a rewarding choice. Real estate is more than just buying and selling properties; it's about helping people find a space that suits their needs, whether that's a family home, a commercial property for a budding business, or a rental property for additional income. It's a career that offers flexibility, financial rewards, and the opportunity to make a real impact on people's lives.

What This Book Offers

This book is designed to be a one-stop-shop for all your Missouri real estate exam needs. We'll start by exploring the Missouri real estate market, giving you a solid grounding in the state-specific aspects you'll need to be familiar with. From there, we'll delve into the eligibility criteria and the application process, ensuring you know exactly what steps you need to take to sit for the exam.

We'll also provide a detailed overview of the exam format, so you know what to expect on the day of the test. But we won't stop there. This book also includes in-depth chapters on each of the key areas you'll be tested on, including property ownership, laws of agency, property valuation, and more. Each chapter is designed to provide you with a thorough understanding of the subject matter, complete with practice questions to help you test your knowledge.

Beyond the Exam

While the primary focus of this book is to help you pass the Missouri Real Estate License Exam, we also recognize that your learning shouldn't stop once you've obtained your license. That's why we've included chapters on career development, ethics, and legal considerations, to give you a well-rounded understanding of what a career in real estate truly entails.

Your Path to Success

The journey to becoming a licensed real estate agent in Missouri is challenging but incredibly rewarding. It requires dedication, continuous learning, and a genuine desire to help people. This book is designed to be your companion on this journey, providing you with all the tools you'll need to succeed.

So, are you ready to take the first step towards a fulfilling career in Missouri real estate? Let's get started!

Understanding the Missouri Real Estate Market

The Missouri real estate market is a diverse and dynamic landscape that offers a range of opportunities for both buyers and sellers. Understanding the intricacies of this market is crucial for anyone aspiring to become a licensed real estate agent in the state. This chapter aims to provide a comprehensive overview of the Missouri real estate market, covering its key characteristics, the factors that influence it, and the trends that are shaping its future.

Geographic Diversity

Missouri is a state of contrasts, geographically speaking. From the bustling urban centers of St. Louis and Kansas City to the serene landscapes of the Ozarks, the state offers a variety of settings that cater to different lifestyles and preferences. This geographic diversity impacts the real estate market in several ways:

Urban Areas

- *St. Louis:* Known for its iconic Gateway Arch, St. Louis is a major cultural and economic hub. The real estate market here is diverse, offering everything from historic homes to modern condos.

- *Kansas City:* Famous for its barbecue and jazz heritage, Kansas City has a robust real estate market characterized by affordable housing and a growing number of luxury properties.

Suburban Communities

Suburbs around major cities like Chesterfield near St. Louis or Overland Park near Kansas City are experiencing growth. These areas offer a mix of residential options, from single-family homes to townhouses and condos.

Rural Areas

Rural Missouri offers vast tracts of agricultural land and small-town living. Properties here are generally more affordable but come with their own set of challenges, such as fewer amenities and longer commutes.

Economic Factors

Employment

Job growth and employment rates are significant indicators of a healthy real estate market. Cities like St. Louis and Kansas City are home to several Fortune 500 companies, providing stable employment opportunities that attract a steady influx of new residents.

Interest Rates

Interest rates set by the Federal Reserve have a direct impact on mortgage rates. Lower interest rates generally stimulate home buying activity, while higher rates can cool the market.

Market Trends

Housing Affordability

Missouri is generally considered an affordable state to live in, especially when compared to coastal states. However, affordability can vary widely depending on the area.

Technology and Real Estate

The rise of real estate technology, including online listings and virtual tours, is changing the way agents and clients interact. Being tech-savvy is increasingly important for success in the market.

Investment Properties

With its affordable property prices, Missouri is becoming a hotspot for real estate investments, including rental properties and fix-and-flip ventures.

Government Policies

Zoning Laws

Understanding zoning laws is crucial for any real estate agent. These laws can affect property usage, from residential and commercial to agricultural.

Tax Incentives

Various tax incentives for first-time homebuyers and property investors can significantly impact the real estate market. Being knowledgeable about these can give you an edge as an agent.

Seasonal Variations

Like many markets, Missouri's real estate activity is subject to seasonal variations. Spring and summer are generally the most active seasons for buying and selling, while activity tends to slow down in the fall and winter.

Challenges and Opportunities

Aging Infrastructure

In some areas, particularly older neighborhoods in cities like St. Louis, aging infrastructure can be a concern for potential buyers.

Urban Renewal

Several Missouri cities are undergoing urban renewal projects, offering opportunities for investment in up-and-coming areas.

Conclusion

Understanding the Missouri real estate market is a complex but rewarding endeavor. From the diverse geographic settings to the economic factors and government policies that influence it, this market offers a range of opportunities and challenges for real estate professionals. Keeping an eye on market trends and being aware of the factors that influence them will equip you with the knowledge you need to succeed in this exciting field.

By grasping the intricacies of the Missouri real estate market, you'll be better prepared to serve your clients' needs, whether they're looking for a downtown loft, a suburban family home, or a rural retreat. So, as you embark on your journey to becoming a licensed real estate agent in Missouri, keep these insights in mind—they'll serve you well in your burgeoning career.

Eligibility Criteria

Becoming a licensed real estate agent in Missouri is a multi-step process that requires meeting specific eligibility criteria. This chapter aims to provide a comprehensive guide to understanding these criteria, from educational requirements to background checks and everything in between. Knowing what is expected of you can significantly streamline your journey to becoming a licensed professional.

Age Requirements

Minimum Age

In Missouri, the minimum age to apply for a real estate license is 18 years. This is a standard requirement across many states and is non-negotiable.

Educational Requirements

Pre-License Education

Before you can apply for a real estate license in Missouri, you must complete a pre-license education course. This course is typically 48 hours long and covers the fundamentals of real estate practice and law.

Course Content

The pre-license course will cover a variety of topics, including:

- Real Estate Law
- Contract Law
- Principles of Marketing

- Ethics and Professional Conduct
- Property Management

Accredited Institutions

It's crucial to ensure that the institution offering the pre-license course is accredited by the Missouri Real Estate Commission. Failure to do so could result in your application being rejected.

Examination Requirements

The Missouri Real Estate Exam

After completing your pre-license education, the next step is to pass the Missouri Real Estate Exam. This exam tests your knowledge on a range of topics, including:

- Real Estate Law and Regulations
- Property Valuation
- Contracts and Agreements
- Ethics and Professional Conduct

Exam Format

The exam is typically divided into two sections: the national portion and the state-specific portion. You must pass both sections to obtain your license.

Exam Fees

There is a fee associated with taking the Missouri Real Estate Exam, which is non-refundable. Make sure to check the most current fees on the Missouri Real Estate Commission's website.

Background Check and Fingerprinting

Criminal Background Check

Missouri requires all applicants to undergo a criminal background check. This is to ensure that you meet the ethical and professional standards expected of a real estate agent.

Fingerprinting

Along with the background check, you'll also need to submit fingerprints for identification. These are usually taken electronically and sent to the Missouri State Highway Patrol and the FBI for processing.

Financial Stability

Credit Score

While not a formal requirement, your credit score may be considered as part of your application. A poor credit score could raise red flags, although it is generally not a disqualifying factor.

Experience

No Prior Experience Required

One of the benefits of becoming a real estate agent in Missouri is that no prior experience is required. However, some brokerages may have their own experience or educational criteria for hiring new agents.

Application Process

Submitting Your Application

Once you meet all the eligibility criteria, the next step is to submit your application to the Missouri Real Estate Commission. This usually involves:

- Filling out the application form
- Submitting proof of education
- Paying the application fee
- Attaching your background check and fingerprinting results

Application Review

After submission, your application will be reviewed by the Commission. This can take several weeks, so it's advisable to apply well in advance of when you hope to start working.

Special Cases

Reciprocity

Missouri has reciprocity agreements with some states, allowing licensed agents from those states to become licensed in Missouri without going through the entire process again. However, they must still meet specific criteria and may need to pass the state portion of the Missouri Real Estate Exam.

License Reinstatement

If you've had a license in the past that has lapsed or been revoked, the process for reinstatement will depend on the circumstances of the lapse or revocation. You may need to retake the pre-license course or the state exam.

Conclusion

Meeting the eligibility criteria to become a licensed real estate agent in Missouri is a rigorous but straightforward process. From age and educational requirements to background checks and exams, each step is designed to ensure that you are well-prepared for a successful career in real estate. By understanding and fulfilling these criteria, you are well on your way to becoming a knowledgeable and ethical real estate professional in the state of Missouri.

Application Process

The application process for obtaining a real estate license in Missouri is a critical phase that requires meticulous attention to detail. This chapter aims to provide a comprehensive, step-by-step guide to navigating this complex process, from the initial application to the final approval. By the end of this chapter, you should have a clear understanding of what to expect and how to prepare for each stage of the application process.

Preparing for the Application

Documentation

Before you even start filling out the application form, gather all the necessary documents. These typically include:

- Proof of age (usually a government-issued ID)
- Educational certificates
- Background check reports
- Fingerprinting results
- Proof of legal residency or citizenship

Application Fees

Be prepared to pay the non-refundable application fee. The fee varies, so it's essential to check the Missouri Real Estate Commission's website for the most current information.

Pre-License Course Completion Certificate

You must have successfully completed the pre-license course from an accredited institution and have a certificate as proof.

The Application Form

Where to Find It

The application form can usually be downloaded from the Missouri Real Estate Commission's website or obtained from their office.

Sections of the Form

The form is divided into several sections, each requiring specific information:

1. Personal Information: This includes your full name, address, and contact details.
2. Educational Background: Here, you'll list your educational qualifications, including the pre-license course.
3. Work Experience: While not mandatory, any relevant work experience can be added here.
4. Legal Information: This section asks about any criminal history or past disciplinary actions.
5. References: Some forms may require professional references.

Filling Out the Form

- *Accuracy:* Ensure all the information is accurate. Any discrepancies can lead to delays or even disqualification.
- *Completeness:* Fill out all required fields. An incomplete application is usually not processed.
- *Legibility:* If filling out by hand, ensure your writing is legible. Illegible forms may be returned.

Submission of the Application

Online vs. Mail

Some states allow online submission, while others require mailing the physical form. Check the Missouri Real Estate Commission's guidelines for the most current information.

What to Include

When submitting, make sure to include:

- The completed application form
- All required documents
- The application fee

Tracking Your Application

It's advisable to send your application via registered mail or use a tracking feature if applying online. This allows you to confirm its receipt.

The Review Process

Initial Review

Once received, the Commission will conduct an initial review to ensure completeness and accuracy. This can take several weeks.

Background Check Verification

The Commission will verify the background check and fingerprinting results you've submitted.

Educational Verification

Your educational certificates and pre-license course completion will also be verified during this stage.

Additional Documentation

In some cases, the Commission may request additional documents or clarifications. Promptly attending to these requests can expedite the process.

The Interview and Examination

Interview

Some states require an interview as part of the application process. If applicable, prepare by reviewing common questions and understanding the Commission's expectations.

Examination

If you haven't already taken the licensing exam, you'll be scheduled for it at this stage. Passing is crucial for moving forward.

Approval and License Issuance

Notification

Once all stages are successfully completed, you'll receive a notification of approval.

Receiving Your License

Your real estate license will be mailed to you, or you may be required to pick it up in person.

Activation

Some licenses need to be activated before they become valid. This usually involves contacting the Commission and confirming your start date.

Common Pitfalls and How to Avoid Them

Incomplete Applications

Always double-check to ensure all fields are filled out and all required documents are attached.

Missed Deadlines

Keep track of all deadlines, including those for submitting additional documents or fees.

Incorrect Information

Double-check all entries for accuracy. Incorrect information can lead to delays or disqualification.

Conclusion

The application process for obtaining a Missouri real estate license may seem daunting, but with careful preparation and attention to detail, it's entirely manageable. This chapter has aimed to provide a comprehensive overview of each stage of the process, from initial preparation to final approval. By following these guidelines, you're well on your way to becoming a licensed real estate agent in Missouri. Good luck on your journey to a fulfilling career in real estate!

Exam Format

The real estate licensing exam is a pivotal moment in your journey to becoming a licensed real estate agent in Missouri. This chapter aims to provide an in-depth look at the exam format, the types of questions you'll encounter, and the strategies you can employ to maximize your chances of success. By the end of this chapter, you should have a comprehensive understanding of what to expect and how to prepare for the Missouri Real Estate License Exam.

Overview of the Exam

Purpose

The primary purpose of the exam is to assess your understanding of real estate principles, laws, and ethical considerations relevant to the Missouri real estate market. The exam ensures that only qualified individuals enter the profession, thereby maintaining the industry's integrity.

Structure

The Missouri Real Estate License Exam is divided into two main sections:

1. National Portion: This section covers general real estate principles and practices applicable across the United States.
2. State-Specific Portion: This section focuses on laws, regulations, and practices unique to Missouri.

Duration and Number of Questions

- *National Portion:* 80 questions, 120 minutes
- *State-Specific Portion:* 40 questions, 60 minutes

Scoring

Each section is scored separately, and you must pass both to obtain your license. The passing score varies, so it's crucial to check the most current information from the Missouri Real Estate Commission.

Types of Questions

Multiple-Choice Questions (MCQs)

The exam consists entirely of multiple-choice questions, each with four answer options. These questions assess your knowledge, comprehension, and application skills.

Categories

Questions in the National Portion are generally categorized into:

1. Property Ownership and Land Use Controls
2. Laws of Agency
3. Valuation and Market Analysis
4. Financing
5. Transfer of Property
6. Practice of Real Estate
7. Contracts

The State-Specific Portion focuses on:

1. State Laws and Regulations
2. Licensing Requirements
3. Statutory Requirements Governing the Activities of Licenses

Strategies for Answering Questions

Elimination Technique

If you're unsure about an answer, try eliminating the least likely options first. This narrows down your choices and increases your chances of selecting the correct answer.

Time Management

You have approximately 1.5 minutes per question in the National Portion and 1.5 minutes per question in the State-Specific Portion. Keep an eye on the clock to ensure you have enough time to answer all questions.

Guessing

If you're completely stumped, it's better to guess than to leave a question blank. There's no penalty for guessing.

Flagging for Review

Most exam software allows you to flag questions for review. Use this feature to mark questions you're unsure about and revisit them if time permits.

Preparing for the Exam

Study Materials

- *Textbooks:* Your pre-license course textbooks are invaluable resources.
- *Online Resources:* Websites, apps, and online courses can supplement your learning.
- *Practice Exams:* These help you get accustomed to the exam format and question types.

Study Plan

1. Initial Assessment: Take a practice exam to identify your strengths and weaknesses.

2. *Focused Study:* Concentrate on areas where you scored lower.

3. Review and Practice: Regularly review all topics and take additional practice exams.

Group Study

Studying with peers can provide different perspectives and make the learning process more engaging.

Day Before the Exam

- *Review:* Go through your notes and any summaries you've made.
- *Rest:* A well-rested mind performs better than a fatigued one.

Day of the Exam

- *Arrive Early:* Aim to arrive at least 30 minutes before the exam starts.
- *Bring Required Items:* Typically, you'll need a government-issued ID and your exam confirmation.
- *Dress Comfortably:* Wear comfortable clothing suitable for a range of temperatures.

After the Exam

Score Report

You'll usually receive your score report immediately after completing the exam. It will indicate whether you've passed or failed each portion.

Next Steps

If you pass, the next steps involve submitting any remaining documents to the Missouri Real Estate Commission and receiving your license. If you fail, you'll receive information on how to retake the exam.

Conclusion

The Missouri Real Estate License Exam is a comprehensive test that requires thorough preparation. Understanding the exam format and the types of questions you'll encounter is crucial for success. This chapter has aimed to provide a detailed guide to help you navigate the exam confidently. Remember, preparation is key, and knowing what to expect is half the battle. Good luck!

Property Ownership and Land Use Controls

Understanding the intricacies of property ownership and land use controls is a cornerstone of real estate practice in Missouri. This chapter aims to provide a comprehensive guide to property ownership and land use controls, covering everything from the types of property and forms of ownership to the various regulations that govern land use in Missouri.

Types of Property

Real Property

Real property, also known as real estate, includes land and anything permanently attached to it, such as buildings, trees, and minerals. In Missouri, real property is subject to property taxes, and the rights to it can be transferred or leased.

Subcategories of Real Property

1. **Residential:** Includes single-family homes, apartments, and condominiums.
2. **Commercial:** Includes office buildings, shopping centers, and hotels.
3. **Industrial:** Includes factories, warehouses, and manufacturing facilities.
4. **Agricultural:** Includes farmland, ranches, and orchards.

Personal Property

Personal property is movable and not permanently attached to land. Examples include furniture, vehicles, and jewelry. In Missouri, personal property is also subject to taxation but at different rates than real property.

Chattels

Chattels are items of personal property like furniture and appliances. They can be "real" chattels, which are used with real property, or "personal" chattels, which are used with the person.

Fixture

A fixture is an item that was once personal property but has been so affixed to land or a building that it becomes part of the real property. The legal test for a fixture includes the method of attachment, adaptability, and intention.

Forms of Property Ownership

Fee Simple Absolute

This is the most complete form of ownership, giving the owner full control over the property, subject to government restrictions like zoning and taxation.

Rights Included

1. **Right of Possession:** The owner has the right to occupy the property.
2. **Right of Control:** The owner can determine the use of the property.
3. **Right of Exclusion:** The owner can decide who may or may not enter the property.
4. **Right of Enjoyment:** The owner can use the property in any legal manner.
5. **Right of Disposition:** The owner can sell, will, or transfer the property.

Life Estate

A life estate grants ownership rights for the duration of a person's life. Upon their death, the property reverts to the original owner or a designated third party. This form is less common but still exists in Missouri, often used for estate planning purposes.

Pur Autre Vie

This is a life estate that is based on the life of a third party. It's a unique form of ownership that ends when a named individual dies.

Leasehold Estate

This is a property interest for a set period, usually defined by the terms of a lease. The lessee has the right to occupy and use the property but does not own it. In Missouri, leasehold estates are subject to the state's landlord-tenant laws.

Types of Leasehold Estates

1. **Estate for Years:** A lease for a specific period.
2. **Estate from Period to Period:** A lease with no defined end date but a recurring period.
3. **Estate at Will:** A lease that can be terminated by either party at any time.
4. **Estate at Sufferance:** A lease where the tenant remains after the lease has ended.

Concurrent Ownership

This refers to property owned by more than one person. Types include:

1. **Joint Tenancy:** Equal ownership and includes the right of survivorship. In Missouri, joint tenancy must be explicitly stated in the deed.
2. **Tenancy in Common:** Unequal ownership and no right of survivorship. This is the default form of concurrent ownership in Missouri.
3. **Tenancy by the Entirety:** Similar to joint tenancy but only for married couples. This form of ownership provides significant protections against creditors in Missouri.

Land Use Controls

Zoning

Zoning laws in Missouri regulate how property in specific geographic zones can be used. Types of zones include residential, commercial, industrial, and agricultural. Zoning is typically controlled by local governments and can vary widely even within the same city.

Zoning Appeals

If a property owner wants to use their property in a way that is not permitted under current zoning laws, they can appeal for a variance or a rezoning. This is a complex process that often requires legal assistance.

Building Codes

Missouri has a set of building codes that specify the minimum acceptable levels of safety for constructed objects like buildings. These codes cover everything from electrical and plumbing systems to fire safety and structural integrity.

Permits and Inspections

Before constructing or significantly altering a building, a property owner must usually obtain a building permit from the local government. Inspections are often required before, during, and after construction.

Environmental Restrictions

Missouri is home to various natural resources, and laws like the Clean Water Act or Endangered Species Act can restrict property use. For example, properties near water bodies may be subject to additional regulations to protect against water pollution.

Eminent Domain

In Missouri, the government has the right to take private property for public use, but they must provide just compensation to the owner. This process is governed by both state and federal laws.

Restrictive Covenants and Homeowners Associations

These are private agreements that restrict the use of land. They are often used in planned communities and subdivisions. In Missouri, these covenants are generally enforceable as long as they are not discriminatory or violate public policy.

Missouri-Specific Regulations

Missouri Clean Water Law

This law regulates water pollution and impacts properties near water bodies. It requires permits for discharging pollutants into state waters.

Farmland Preservation

Missouri has several programs aimed at preserving agricultural land. These programs can affect how such properties can be converted to other uses.

Historic Preservation

Properties located in historic districts in Missouri may be subject to additional restrictions and could be eligible for tax incentives.

Missouri Human Rights Act

This act prohibits discrimination in housing and is specific to Missouri. It covers more types of discrimination than the federal Fair Housing Act.

Legal Procedures in Property Ownership

Title Search and Insurance

Before purchasing a property, a title search is usually conducted to ensure that the seller has a clear title to the property. Title insurance protects against future claims against the property.

The Closing Process

This is the final step in a real estate transaction where ownership is transferred from the seller to the buyer. In Missouri, closings are typically conducted by a title company or attorney.

Tax Implications

Property Taxes

In Missouri, property taxes are a significant source of revenue for local governments. These taxes are based on the assessed value of the property.

Capital Gains Tax

If you sell a property in Missouri that has increased in value, you may be subject to capital gains tax. However, there are exemptions available for primary residences.

Ethical Considerations

Fair Housing Act

This federal law prohibits discrimination in the sale, rental, and financing of dwellings based on race, color, national origin, religion, sex, familial status, and disability.

Missouri Human Rights Act

This act also prohibits discrimination in housing but is specific to Missouri. It covers more types of discrimination than the federal Fair Housing Act.

Conclusion

Understanding property ownership and land use controls is a complex but crucial aspect of real estate practice in Missouri. This chapter aimed to provide a comprehensive overview to equip you with the knowledge you need to navigate this intricate landscape. Whether you're advising clients, making a sale, or managing properties, the information in this chapter will serve as an invaluable resource.

By mastering the concepts in this chapter, you're not just preparing for the Missouri Real Estate License Exam; you're laying the foundation for a successful career in real estate. Keep learning, stay updated with the latest laws and regulations, and always practice ethically. Your future in real estate looks promising.

Mock Exam Property Ownership and Land Use Controls

➙1. What is the most complete form of ownership?

   A. Life Estate
   B. Leasehold Estate
   C. Fee Simple Absolute
   D. Joint Tenancy

Answer: C. Fee Simple Absolute

Fee Simple Absolute grants the owner all rights to the property, including the ability to sell, lease, or will it to heirs.

➙2. What does a life estate provide?

   A. Complete control of the property
   B. Ownership for the duration of someone's life
   C. Equal ownership among spouses
   D. Ownership for a specified period

Answer: B. Ownership for the duration of someone's life

A life estate grants ownership for the duration of someone's life, usually the life tenant. Upon their death, the property reverts to the original owner or a designated remainderman.

➙3. What is the primary advantage of a Leasehold Estate?

   A. Equity build-up
   B. Lower upfront costs
   C. Complete control
   D. Right of survivorship

Answer: B. Lower upfront costs

The primary advantage of a Leasehold Estate is lower upfront costs. The tenant has the right to occupy and use the property for a specified period, but ownership remains with the landlord.

➡ 4. What is unique about Joint Tenancy?

A. Unequal shares
B. No right of survivorship
C. Equal shares and right of survivorship
D. Complete control of the property

Answer: C. Equal shares and right of survivorship

Joint tenancy involves two or more people owning property with equal shares and the right of survivorship.

➡ 5. In which states is Community Property a common form of ownership?

A. All states
B. Only in community property states
C. Only in common law states
D. None of the above

Answer: B. Only in community property states

Community Property is a form of ownership common in community property states, where any property acquired during a marriage is considered jointly owned by both spouses.

➡ 6. What is the primary purpose of zoning laws?

A. To control property taxes
B. To regulate land use

C. To establish school districts

D. To determine property value

Answer: B. To regulate land use

Zoning laws are enacted by local governments to regulate how land can be used in specific areas.

7. What is eminent domain?

A. The right to lease property

B. The right of the government to take private property for public use

C. The right to inherit property

D. The right to sell property

Answer: B. The right of the government to take private property for public use

Eminent domain is the power of the government to take private property for public use, usually with compensation to the owner.

8. What is a variance in the context of land use?

A. A change in property value

B. A change in zoning laws

C. Permission to use land in a way that is prohibited by zoning laws

D. A change in property taxes

Answer: C. Permission to use land in a way that is prohibited by zoning laws

A variance is special permission granted by a zoning authority to use land in a manner that is generally not allowed under current zoning laws.

9. What is a restrictive covenant?

A. A government-imposed restriction on land use

B. A privately imposed agreement that restricts the use of land

C. A restriction on the sale of property

D. A restriction on leasing property

Answer: B. A privately imposed agreement that restricts the use of land

A restrictive covenant is an agreement that limits how a property owner can use their property, usually to preserve the value and integrity of a neighborhood.

10. What is the difference between real property and personal property?

A. Real property can be moved, but personal property cannot

B. Real property is land and anything permanently attached to it, while personal property is movable

C. Real property is always more valuable

D. There is no difference

Answer: B. Real property is land and anything permanently attached to it, while personal property is movable

Real property refers to land and anything permanently attached to it, like buildings. Personal property refers to movable items like furniture and cars.

11. What is a buffer zone in land use planning?

A. An area between residential and commercial zones

B. An area reserved for parks

C. An area where any type of construction is allowed

D. An area reserved for schools

Answer: A. An area between residential and commercial zones

A buffer zone is an area that separates different types of land uses, like residential and commercial, to reduce conflict between them.

12. What is the main goal of sustainable development?

A. To maximize profits
B. To use resources in a way that meets current needs without compromising future needs
C. To develop as quickly as possible
D. To use all available land

Answer: B. To use resources in a way that meets current needs without compromising future needs

Sustainable development aims to meet the needs of the present without compromising the ability of future generations to meet their own needs.

13. What is a master plan in the context of city planning?

A. A detailed budget
B. A long-term planning document that guides future growth and development
C. A short-term plan for immediate construction
D. A plan for a single building

Answer: B. A long-term planning document that guides future growth and development

A master plan is a comprehensive long-term plan that outlines the vision, policies, and goals for future growth and development in a city or community.

14. What is the main purpose of a building permit?

A. To raise revenue for the city
B. To ensure that construction complies with local codes and ordinances
C. To limit the number of buildings in an area
D. To increase property values

Answer: B. To ensure that construction complies with local codes and ordinances

A building permit is required to ensure that any new construction or significant changes to existing structures comply with local building codes and regulations.

15. What is the role of a property appraiser in land use?

A. To determine the highest and best use of a property
B. To enforce zoning laws
C. To issue building permits
D. To draft master plans

Answer: A. To determine the highest and best use of a property

A property appraiser assesses the value of a property based on its highest and best use, considering factors like location, zoning, and market conditions.

16. What is the "Right to Farm" law?

A. A law that allows anyone to farm anywhere
B. A law that protects farmers from nuisance lawsuits
C. A law that restricts farming to certain zones
D. A law that bans farming in urban areas

Answer: B. A law that protects farmers from nuisance lawsuits

The "Right to Farm" law is designed to protect existing farmers from nuisance lawsuits filed by new neighbors who may not be accustomed to the operations of a farm.

17. What does the term "infill development" refer to?

A. Developing farmland into residential areas
B. Developing open spaces in urban areas
C. Developing new structures on vacant or underused land within existing city boundaries
D. Expanding urban areas into rural zones

Answer: C. Developing new structures on vacant or underused land within existing city boundaries

Infill development aims to make use of vacant or underutilized lands within a built-up area for further construction or development.

➡ 18. What is a nonconforming use?

A. A use that conforms to current zoning laws but not to building codes
B. A use that was lawful before a zoning ordinance was passed but is no longer permitted
C. A use that violates both zoning laws and building codes
D. A use that is temporarily permitted due to a variance

Answer: B. A use that was lawful before a zoning ordinance was passed but is no longer permitted

A nonconforming use is a land use that was legal when established but does not conform to new or changed zoning laws.

➡ 19. What is the main purpose of a land trust?

A. To hold land for development
B. To preserve land for future generations
C. To generate revenue through land sales
D. To control land prices

Answer: B. To preserve land for future generations

A land trust is an organization that actively works to conserve land by undertaking or assisting in land or conservation easement acquisition.

➡ 20. What is "mixed-use development"?

A. Development that includes both residential and commercial properties
B. Development that is used for industrial purposes

C. Development that is only used for residential purposes

D. Development that is only used for commercial purposes

Answer: A. Development that includes both residential and commercial properties

Mixed-use development is a type of urban development that blends residential, commercial, cultural, institutional, or entertainment uses.

➡ 21. What is the primary purpose of a greenbelt?

A. To provide recreational spaces

B. To separate urban areas from rural areas

C. To increase property values

D. To reduce air pollution

Answer: B. To separate urban areas from rural areas

A greenbelt is an area of largely undeveloped, wild, or agricultural land surrounding or neighboring urban areas.

➡ 22. What is "brownfield land"?

A. Land that is used for agricultural purposes

B. Land that has been contaminated by hazardous waste

C. Land that is reserved for parks and recreation

D. Land that is zoned for industrial use

Answer: B. Land that has been contaminated by hazardous waste

Brownfield land is a term used in urban planning to describe any previously developed land that is not currently in use and may be potentially contaminated.

➡ 23. What does "highest and best use" mean in the context of real estate?

A. The use that generates the most income

B. The use that is most suitable from a social perspective

C. The use that maximizes a property's value

D. The use that is most environmentally sustainable

Answer: C. The use that maximizes a property's value

"Highest and best use" is a real estate appraisal term for the most profitable, likely use of a property, which is physically possible, appropriately supported, and legally permissible.

➡ 24. What is "air rights"?

A. The right to unlimited views from a property

B. The right to the air above the land

C. The right to pollute the air

D. The right to fresh air

Answer: B. The right to the air above the land

Air rights are a type of development right in real estate, referring to the empty space above a property.

➡ 25. What is "land banking"?

A. The process of buying land as an investment

B. The process of rezoning land

C. The process of converting agricultural land to residential land

D. The process of accumulating land for future development

Answer: D. The process of accumulating land for future development

Land banking is the practice of aggregating parcels of land for future sale or development.

➡ 26. What is "eminent domain"?

A. The right of the government to tax property

B. The right of the government to seize private property for public use

C. The right of the property owner to change the zoning laws

D. The right of the property owner to deny access to government officials

Answer: B. The right of the government to seize private property for public use

Eminent domain is the power of the government to take private property and convert it into public use, often with compensation to the owner.

➡ 27. What is "spot zoning"?

A. Zoning that changes frequently

B. Zoning that applies to a specific area within a larger zoned area

C. Zoning that applies only to commercial properties

D. Zoning that applies only during certain times of the year

Answer: B. Zoning that applies to a specific area within a larger zoned area

Spot zoning is the application of zoning laws that are different from the surrounding area, usually benefiting a single property owner.

➡ 28. What does "buffer zone" mean in the context of land use?

A. An area that separates different types of land uses

B. An area that is restricted for military use

C. An area that is designated for future development

D. An area that is kept empty for aesthetic purposes

Answer: A. An area that separates different types of land uses

A buffer zone is a zonal area that lies between two or more other areas that are contrasting in nature.

➡ 29. What is "downzoning"?

A. Changing the zoning of a property to a less intensive use
B. Changing the zoning of a property to a more intensive use
C. Rezoning to allow for higher buildings
D. Rezoning to allow for commercial use

Answer: A. Changing the zoning of a property to a less intensive use
Downzoning is the rezoning of land to a more restrictive zone to prevent overdevelopment.

➡ 30. What is "land grading"?

A. The process of making land more level
B. The process of evaluating the quality of soil
C. The process of determining the value of the land
D. The process of rezoning land

Answer: A. The process of making land more level
Land grading is the act of leveling the surface of the soil to prepare it for construction or agriculture.

➡ 31. What is "land reclamation"?

A. The process of converting developed land back to its natural state
B. The process of converting barren land into arable land
C. The process of restoring contaminated land
D. All of the above

Answer: D. All of the above
Land reclamation can involve converting barren land into arable land, restoring contaminated land, or converting developed land back to its natural state.

➡ 32. What is "land tenure"?

A. The legal regime in which land is owned

B. The length of time land has been owned by a single entity

C. The tax status of a piece of land

D. The zoning classification of a piece of land

Answer: A. The legal regime in which land is owned

Land tenure is the way land is held or owned at the individual or collective level.

➡ 33. What is "land partition"?

A. The division of a larger piece of land into smaller lots

B. The legal process to settle land disputes

C. The change of land zoning types

D. The process of land reclamation

Answer: A. The division of a larger piece of land into smaller lots

Land partition is the division of real property into two or more parcels.

➡ 34. What is "land speculation"?

A. Buying land with the hope that its value will increase

B. Buying land for immediate development

C. Buying land for long-term investment

D. Buying land for agricultural use

Answer: A. Buying land with the hope that its value will increase

Land speculation is the purchase of land with the hope that it will increase in value for resale at a profit.

➡ 35. What is "land surveying"?

A. The process of measuring land and its features

B. The process of evaluating the quality of soil

C. The process of determining the value of the land

D. The process of rezoning land

Answer: A. The process of measuring land and its features

Land surveying is the technique of determining the terrestrial or three-dimensional position of points and the distances and angles between them.

➙ **36. What is "inclusionary zoning"?**

A. Zoning that includes only residential properties

B. Zoning that mandates a portion of new development be affordable for low-income households

C. Zoning that includes only commercial properties

D. Zoning that includes only industrial properties

Answer: B. Zoning that mandates a portion of new development be affordable for low-income households

Inclusionary zoning is a regulation that requires a given share of new construction to be affordable for people with low to moderate incomes.

➙ **37. What is "land banking"?**

A. The process of buying land for immediate development

B. The process of holding onto land as a long-term investment

C. The process of using land as collateral for a loan

D. The process of converting barren land into arable land

Answer: B. The process of holding onto land as a long-term investment

Land banking is the practice of aggregating parcels of land for future sale or development.

➙ **38. What does "air rights" refer to?**

A. The right to unlimited height in building above a property

B. The right to clean air in a residential area

C. The right to the airspace above the physical property

D. The right to fly drones over a property

Answer: C. The right to the airspace above the physical property

Air rights are the property interest in the "space" above the earth's surface.

39. What is "land assembly"?

A. The process of gathering various small parcels of land into a single larger parcel

B. The process of constructing a building on a piece of land

C. The process of converting barren land into arable land

D. The process of dividing a larger piece of land into smaller lots

Answer: A. The process of gathering various small parcels of land into a single larger parcel

Land assembly is the process by which smaller parcels of land are combined to create a single larger parcel.

40. What is "land degradation"?

A. The process of land losing its productivity due to human activities

B. The process of land increasing in value

C. The process of land being rezoned for less intensive use

D. The process of land being converted into a natural reserve

Answer: A. The process of land losing its productivity due to human activities

Land degradation refers to the deterioration or loss of the productive capacity of the soils for present and future.

41. What is "land improvement"?

A. The process of adding value to a land through developments like roads and utilities

B. The process of converting barren land into arable land

C. The process of rezoning land for more intensive use

D. The process of restoring contaminated land

Answer: A. The process of adding value to a land through developments like roads and utilities

Land improvement refers to the effort made to make land more usable and valuable.

42. What is "land lease"?

A. A contract where the landowner gives another the right to use land in exchange for rent

B. A contract to sell land

C. A contract to buy land

D. A contract to develop land

Answer: A. A contract where the landowner gives another the right to use land in exchange for rent

A land lease is an agreement where the landowner permits a tenant to use the land in exchange for rent.

43. What is "land reservation"?

A. Land set aside for future use

B. Land set aside for indigenous people

C. Land set aside for environmental protection

D. All of the above

Answer: D. All of the above

Land reservation can refer to land set aside for various purposes, including future use, protection of indigenous rights, or environmental conservation.

44. What is "land trust"?

A. A legal entity that holds the ownership of a land for the benefit of another party
B. A company that invests in land
C. A non-profit organization that protects land for future generations
D. A government agency that manages public lands

Answer: A. A legal entity that holds the ownership of a land for the benefit of another party

A land trust is a legal entity that takes ownership of, or authority over, a property at the behest of the property owner.

45. What is "land use planning"?

A. The process of managing land resources to prevent land degradation
B. The process of determining the best way to use land resources
C. The process of rezoning land
D. The process of converting barren land into arable land

Answer: B. The process of determining the best way to use land resources

Land use planning involves the systematic assessment of land and water potential, alternatives for land use, and the economic and social conditions.

46. What does "eminent domain" refer to?

A. The right of the government to take private property for public use
B. The right of a landlord to evict a tenant for non-payment of rent
C. The right of a property owner to develop their land as they see fit
D. The right of a tenant to enjoy their rented property without interference from the landlord

Answer: A. The right of the government to take private property for public use

Eminent domain is the power of the government to take private property and convert it into public use, usually with compensation to the owner.

47. What is "adverse possession"?

A. The illegal occupation of property
B. The acquisition of property through inheritance
C. The acquisition of property through a long-term, open, and notorious occupation
D. The acquisition of property through a legal purchase

Answer: C. The acquisition of property through a long-term, open, and notorious occupation

Adverse possession is a legal principle that allows a person who possesses someone else's land for an extended period of time to claim legal title to that land.

48. What is "land value tax"?

A. A tax on the value of a building
B. A tax on the value of land, excluding the value of buildings and improvements
C. A tax on the sale of land
D. A tax on the rental income from land

Answer: B. A tax on the value of land, excluding the value of buildings and improvements

A land value tax is a levy on the unimproved value of land.

49. What is "landlocked property"?

A. Property that is surrounded by other properties, with no direct access to a public road
B. Property that is located far from any body of water
C. Property that is not subject to flooding
D. Property that is restricted from development

Answer: A. Property that is surrounded by other properties, with no direct access to a public road

Landlocked property is real estate that has no direct access to a public street, so you can't get to it unless you go through someone else's property first.

➡ 50. What is "latent defect"?

A. A defect that is obvious and easy to spot
B. A defect that is hidden and not immediately obvious
C. A defect that has been disclosed by the seller
D. A defect that has been repaired before the sale of the property

Answer: B. A defect that is hidden and not immediately obvious

A latent defect is a fault in the property that could not have been discovered by a reasonably thorough inspection before the sale.

Laws of Agency and Fiduciary Duties

Navigating the complex world of real estate transactions requires a deep understanding of the laws of agency and fiduciary duties. This chapter aims to provide a comprehensive guide to these critical aspects of real estate practice in Missouri, covering everything from the types of agency relationships to the ethical and legal responsibilities that come with them.

Types of Agency Relationships

Universal Agent

A universal agent has broad authority to act on behalf of the principal in all matters, both business and personal. This type of agency is rare in real estate transactions.

General Agent

A general agent has the power to act on behalf of the principal in a specific range of matters. For example, a property manager is a general agent for the property owner.

Special Agent

A special agent, also known as a limited agent, has authority to perform specific acts for the principal. Real estate agents are typically special agents authorized to represent clients in property transactions.

Dual Agency

In dual agency, the agent represents both the buyer and the seller in the same transaction. Missouri law allows dual agency but requires informed consent from all parties.

Designated Agency

In this arrangement, different agents from the same brokerage represent the buyer and the seller, avoiding the conflicts of interest inherent in dual agency.

Subagency

In subagency, one agent delegates part of their duties to another agent. The subagent owes fiduciary duties to the principal of the original agent.

Fiduciary Duties

Duty of Loyalty

The agent must act in the best interest of the principal, even over their own interests. This includes disclosing any conflicts of interest and not taking advantage of the principal for personal gain.

Duty of Obedience

The agent must follow all lawful instructions from the principal. Failure to do so could result in legal consequences.

Duty of Disclosure

The agent must disclose all material facts that could affect the principal's decision-making. This includes any known defects in the property, as well as any offers from other parties.

Duty of Confidentiality

The agent must keep the principal's personal and financial information confidential, even after the agency relationship has ended.

Duty of Reasonable Care and Diligence

The agent must exercise a reasonable degree of care while representing the principal, which includes doing proper research and providing accurate information.

Duty of Accounting

The agent must account for all funds and property received during the agency relationship. This includes keeping accurate records and not commingling client funds with personal funds.

Missouri-Specific Laws and Regulations

Missouri Broker Disclosure Form

In Missouri, agents are required to provide clients with a broker disclosure form that outlines the types of agency relationships and the duties and responsibilities associated with each.

Written Agreements

Missouri law requires that all agency relationships in real estate transactions be established through written agreements. These agreements must specify the scope of the agent's authority and the duration of the relationship.

Termination of Agency

In Missouri, an agency relationship can be terminated through completion of the transaction, expiration of the agreement, mutual agreement, or breach of fiduciary duties.

Dual Agency Consent

If an agent wishes to represent both the buyer and the seller in a transaction, Missouri law requires that both parties give informed consent, usually through a written agreement.

Ethical Considerations

Code of Ethics

Real estate agents in Missouri are often members of the National Association of Realtors (NAR), which has its own Code of Ethics. This code provides additional guidelines on how agents should conduct themselves, including how to handle conflicts of interest and how to provide equal services to all clients, regardless of race, color, religion, sex, handicap, familial status, or national origin.

Handling of Funds

Ethical guidelines dictate that agents must handle client funds with extreme care, depositing them into an escrow account separate from their personal or business accounts.

Advertising and Representation

Agents must be truthful in advertising and must not misrepresent properties. They should provide accurate information in listings and should not exaggerate or omit material facts.

Legal Consequences of Breach of Duty

Civil Liability

An agent who breaches their fiduciary duties may be held liable for damages. The principal may sue for breach of contract, negligence, or even fraud in extreme cases.

Disciplinary Actions

The Missouri Real Estate Commission can take disciplinary actions against agents who violate state laws or regulations. This can range from fines to revocation of the agent's license.

Criminal Liability

In extreme cases, such as embezzlement or fraud, an agent could face criminal charges, leading to imprisonment.

Conclusion

Understanding the laws of agency and fiduciary duties is crucial for anyone involved in real estate transactions in Missouri. These laws and duties not only govern the ethical and professional conduct of real estate agents but also provide a framework that protects consumers. By adhering to these guidelines, agents can maintain the trust and confidence of their clients, thereby fostering successful and ethical real estate practices.

Whether you're a seasoned agent or a newcomer to the field, this chapter serves as an invaluable resource for understanding the complex landscape of agency laws and fiduciary duties in Missouri. It equips you with the knowledge and tools you need to navigate real estate transactions ethically and legally, setting you up for long-term success in your career.

Mock Exam Laws of Agency and Fiduciary Duties

➡1. What is the primary role of an agent in a real estate transaction?

A. To represent the buyer only
B. To act on behalf of the principal
C. To market the property
D. To negotiate the best price for themselves

Answer: B

The primary role of an agent is to act on behalf of the principal, whether that's the buyer or the seller.

➡2. Which of the following is NOT a fiduciary duty an agent owes to their client?

A. Loyalty
B. Disclosure
C. Profit maximization
D. Confidentiality

Answer: C

Profit maximization is not a fiduciary duty. The fiduciary duties include loyalty, disclosure, and confidentiality among others.

➡3. What is dual agency?

A. When two agents represent a buyer
B. When an agent represents both buyer and seller
C. When two agents represent a seller
D. When an agent represents two buyers

Answer: B

Dual agency occurs when an agent represents both the buyer and the seller in a single transaction.

➡ 4. Which state law is most likely to govern real estate agency relationships?

A. Federal law
B. Common law
C. State-specific law
D. International law

Answer: C

Each state has its own set of laws and regulations governing real estate agency relationships.

➡ 5. What must an agent do if they are involved in a dual agency situation?

A. Keep it a secret
B. Get written consent from both parties
C. Represent the buyer's interests only
D. Represent the seller's interests only

Answer: B

In a dual agency situation, both parties must be made fully aware of the dual agency and consent to it in writing.

➡ 6. What does the fiduciary duty of "reasonable care and skill" entail?

A. Making the most money for the client
B. Acting as any competent agent would
C. Keeping all information confidential
D. Always being available for the client

Answer: B

The duty of "reasonable care and skill" means the agent must act as any competent agent would in the same situation.

➡ 7. What is the primary focus of the fiduciary duty of "loyalty"?

A. Maximizing profit for the agent
B. Putting the client's needs above the agent's
C. Keeping all information confidential
D. Disclosing all facts to the client

Answer: B

The fiduciary duty of "loyalty" requires the agent to always act in the best interest of their client.

➡ 8. What is the consequence of breaching fiduciary duties?

A. Loss of job
B. Legal liabilities
C. A warning
D. No consequences

Answer: B

Breaching fiduciary duties can result in various legal liabilities, including fines and loss of license.

➡ 9. What is the purpose of an agency agreement?

A. To outline the agent's commission
B. To outline the scope of the agent's responsibilities
C. To protect the agent from legal action
D. To list the properties for sale

Answer: B

An agency agreement outlines the scope of the agent's responsibilities and how they will be compensated.

➡10. Which of the following is NOT a type of agency relationship in real estate?

A. Seller's agent
B. Buyer's agent
C. Independent agent
D. Dual agent

Answer: C

"Independent agent" is not a standard type of agency relationship in real estate. The common types are seller's agent, buyer's agent, and dual agent.

➡11. What is the term for the person represented by an agent?

A. Client
B. Customer
C. Broker
D. Associate

Answer: A

The person represented by an agent is referred to as the client.

➡12. What is the fiduciary duty of "disclosure" primarily concerned with?

A. Revealing all known facts that materially affect the property
B. Keeping the client's information confidential
C. Making the most money for the client
D. Always being available for the client

Answer: A

The fiduciary duty of "disclosure" requires the agent to reveal all known facts that materially affect the property's value.

13. What is the opposite of a dual agency?

A. Single agency
B. Triple agency
C. No agency
D. Sub-agency

Answer: A

The opposite of a dual agency is a single agency, where the agent represents only one party in the transaction.

14. What is the primary purpose of a buyer's agent?

A. To represent the seller
B. To represent the buyer
C. To market the property
D. To negotiate the best price for themselves

Answer: B

The primary purpose of a buyer's agent is to represent the buyer's interests in the transaction.

15. What is the fiduciary duty of "obedience" concerned with?

A. Following all of the client's lawful instructions
B. Disclosing all material facts
C. Keeping all information confidential
D. Making the most money for the client

Answer: A

The fiduciary duty of "obedience" requires the agent to follow all lawful instructions from their client.

➡ 16. What is the primary role of a sub-agent?

A. To represent the buyer
B. To represent the seller
C. To assist the primary agent
D. To market the property

Answer: C

The primary role of a sub-agent is to assist the primary agent in fulfilling their duties.

➡ 17. What is the fiduciary duty of "accounting"?

A. Keeping track of all financial transactions
B. Disclosing all material facts
C. Keeping all information confidential
D. Making the most money for the client

Answer: A

The fiduciary duty of "accounting" requires the agent to keep track of all financial transactions related to the agency relationship.

➡ 18. What is the primary purpose of a listing agreement?

A. To outline the buyer's needs
B. To outline the scope of the agent's responsibilities towards the seller
C. To protect the agent from legal action
D. To list the properties for rent

Answer: B

A listing agreement outlines the scope of the agent's responsibilities towards the seller and how they will be compensated.

➡ 19. What is the term for an agent who represents the seller?

A. Buyer's agent
B. Seller's agent
C. Dual agent
D. Sub-agent

Answer: B
An agent who represents the seller is known as a seller's agent.

➡ 20. What is the consequence of not disclosing a dual agency?

A. Loss of job
B. Legal liabilities
C. A warning
D. No consequences

Answer: B
Failure to disclose a dual agency can result in legal liabilities, including fines and loss of license.

➡ 21. What is the primary role of a transaction broker?

A. To represent the buyer
B. To represent the seller
C. To facilitate the transaction without representing either party
D. To market the property

Answer: C
A transaction broker's primary role is to facilitate the real estate transaction without representing either the buyer or the seller.

➡ 22. What does the fiduciary duty of "loyalty" require?

A. Disclosing all material facts
B. Putting the client's interests above all others
C. Keeping all information confidential
D. Following all of the client's instructions

Answer: B
The fiduciary duty of "loyalty" requires the agent to put the client's interests above all others, including their own.

➡ 23. What is the term for an agent who represents both the buyer and the seller in the same transaction?

A. Single agent
B. Dual agent
C. Sub-agent
D. Transaction broker

Answer: B
An agent who represents both the buyer and the seller in the same transaction is known as a dual agent.

➡ 24. What is the fiduciary duty of "reasonable care and diligence" concerned with?

A. Protecting the client's financial interests
B. Disclosing all material facts

C. Keeping all information confidential

D. Following all of the client's instructions

Answer: A

The fiduciary duty of "reasonable care and diligence" requires the agent to protect the client's financial interests in the transaction.

25. What is the term for a written agreement between the agent and the client?

A. Listing agreement

B. Agency agreement

C. Contract

D. Memorandum of understanding

Answer: B

A written agreement between the agent and the client outlining the scope of their relationship is known as an agency agreement.

26. What is the primary purpose of a seller's agent?

A. To represent the buyer

B. To represent the seller

C. To market the property

D. To negotiate the best price for themselves

Answer: B

The primary purpose of a seller's agent is to represent the seller's interests in the transaction.

27. What is the fiduciary duty of "confidentiality" concerned with?

A. Protecting the client's financial interests

B. Disclosing all material facts

C. Keeping all information confidential

D. Following all of the client's instructions

Answer: C

The fiduciary duty of "confidentiality" requires the agent to keep all client information confidential unless required to disclose it by law.

➡ 28. What is the term for an agent who does not represent either party and simply facilitates the transaction?

A. Single agent

B. Dual agent

C. Transaction broker

D. Sub-agent

Answer: C

An agent who does not represent either party and simply facilitates the transaction is known as a transaction broker.

➡ 29. What is the primary purpose of a dual agent?

A. To represent the buyer

B. To represent the seller

C. To represent both the buyer and the seller

D. To market the property

Answer: C

The primary purpose of a dual agent is to represent both the buyer and the seller in the same transaction.

➡ 30. What is the fiduciary duty of "full disclosure" concerned with?

A. Protecting the client's financial interests
B. Disclosing all material facts
C. Keeping all information confidential
D. Following all of the client's instructions

Answer: B

The fiduciary duty of "full disclosure" requires the agent to disclose all material facts that could affect the client's decisions.

➡ 31. What is the term for an agent who represents the buyer exclusively?

A. Buyer's agent
B. Seller's agent
C. Dual agent
D. Transaction broker

Answer: A

A buyer's agent exclusively represents the buyer's interests in a real estate transaction.

➡ 32. What is the term used to describe the agent's responsibility to act in the best interests of the client?

A. Loyalty
B. Obedience
C. Disclosure
D. Confidentiality

Answer: A

The term "loyalty" is used to describe the agent's fiduciary duty to act in the best interests of the client.

33. What is the legal obligation called when an agent must keep the client's information confidential even after the agency relationship has ended?

A. Perpetual confidentiality
B. Eternal secrecy
C. Ongoing disclosure
D. Extended loyalty

Answer: A

The legal obligation is called "perpetual confidentiality," requiring the agent to keep the client's information confidential indefinitely, even after the agency relationship has ended.

34. What does the fiduciary duty of "accounting" require?

A. Keeping accurate financial records
B. Disclosing all material facts
C. Keeping all information confidential
D. Following all of the client's instructions

Answer: A

The fiduciary duty of "accounting" requires the agent to keep accurate financial records related to the transaction.

35. What is the term for a written agreement between a buyer and an agent?

A. Buyer's agreement
B. Listing agreement
C. Agency agreement
D. Purchase agreement

Answer: A

A written agreement between a buyer and an agent is known as a buyer's agreement.

36. What is the primary purpose of a listing agent?

A. To represent the buyer
B. To represent the seller
C. To market the property
D. To negotiate the best price for themselves

Answer: C

The primary purpose of a listing agent is to market the property to potential buyers.

37. What is the fiduciary duty of "disclosure" concerned with?

A. Protecting the client's financial interests
B. Disclosing all material facts
C. Keeping all information confidential
D. Following all of the client's instructions

Answer: B

The fiduciary duty of "disclosure" requires the agent to disclose all material facts that could affect the client's decisions.

38. What is the term for an agent who represents the seller exclusively?

A. Buyer's agent
B. Seller's agent
C. Dual agent
D. Transaction broker

Answer: B

A seller's agent exclusively represents the seller's interests in a real estate transaction.

39. What is the primary role of a dual agent?

A. To represent the buyer
B. To represent the seller
C. To represent both the buyer and the seller
D. To market the property

Answer: C

The primary role of a dual agent is to represent both the buyer and the seller in the same transaction.

40. What is the fiduciary duty of "loyalty" concerned with?

A. Protecting the client's financial interests
B. Disclosing all material facts
C. Keeping all information confidential
D. Putting the client's interests above all others

Answer: D

The fiduciary duty of "loyalty" requires the agent to put the client's interests above all others, including their own.

41. What is the primary purpose of a buyer's agent in a real estate transaction?

A. To represent the seller's interests
B. To represent the buyer's interests
C. To act as a neutral third party
D. To facilitate the transaction without representation

Answer: B

The primary purpose of a buyer's agent is to represent the interests of the buyer in a real estate transaction.

➡ 42. What is the fiduciary duty that requires an agent to be honest and forthright with the client?

A. Loyalty
B. Disclosure
C. Obedience
D. Accountability

Answer: B

The fiduciary duty of disclosure requires an agent to be honest and forthright with the client, providing all relevant information.

➡ 43. What is the term for the legal relationship between a principal and an agent where the agent is expected to represent the principal's interests?

A. Contractual agreement
B. Fiduciary relationship
C. Business partnership
D. Legal guardianship

Answer: B

The term "fiduciary relationship" describes the legal relationship between a principal and an agent, where the agent is expected to represent the principal's interests with the utmost good faith, trust, confidence, and candor.

➡ 44. What is the fiduciary duty that requires an agent to follow all lawful instructions from the client?

A. Obedience
B. Loyalty
C. Disclosure

D. Accountability

Answer: A

The fiduciary duty of obedience requires an agent to follow all lawful instructions given by the client.

➡ 45. What is the term used to describe the agent's responsibility to safeguard the client's financial interests?

A. Accountability
B. Loyalty
C. Disclosure
D. Obedience

Answer: A

The term "accountability" is used to describe the agent's fiduciary duty to safeguard the client's financial interests.

➡ 46. What is the legal obligation called when an agent must disclose any known defects of the property?

A. Material fact disclosure
B. Defect revelation
C. Condition reporting
D. Property transparency

Answer: A

The legal obligation is called "material fact disclosure," requiring the agent to disclose any known defects of the property to the client.

➡ 47. What is the term used to describe the agent's responsibility to keep the client informed at all times?

A. Loyalty
B. Disclosure
C. Obedience
D. Accountability

Answer: B

The term "disclosure" is used to describe the agent's fiduciary duty to keep the client informed at all times.

➡ 48. In a dual agency relationship, what must the agent do to avoid conflicts of interest?

A. Represent only the buyer's interests
B. Represent only the seller's interests
C. Obtain written consent from both parties
D. Avoid disclosing any confidential information to either party

Answer: C

In a dual agency relationship, the agent must obtain written consent from both parties to avoid conflicts of interest. This ensures that both the buyer and the seller are aware of the situation and agree to it.

➡ 49. Which of the following is NOT a duty of an agent towards their client?

A. Confidentiality
B. Obedience
C. Disclosure
D. Independence

Answer: D

Independence is not a duty of an agent towards their client. Agents are expected to act in the best interests of their clients, which includes duties like confidentiality, obedience, and disclosure.

→50. What is the term for a situation where an agent represents both the buyer and the seller in a transaction?

A. Double agency
B. Single agency
C. Sub-agency
D. Non-agency

Answer: A

The term for a situation where an agent represents both the buyer and the seller in a transaction is called "double agency." This situation requires informed consent from both parties and can present a conflict of interest for the agent.

Property Valuation and Financial Analysis

Property valuation and financial analysis are the cornerstones of any successful real estate transaction. Whether you're a buyer, seller, or an agent, understanding the intricacies of these topics can make or break a deal. This chapter aims to provide a comprehensive guide to property valuation and financial analysis in the context of the Missouri real estate market.

Property Valuation Methods

Comparative Market Analysis (CMA)

The most common method used in residential real estate, CMA involves comparing the property in question to similar properties that have recently sold, are currently on the market, or were listed but did not sell. Factors like location, size, condition, and amenities are considered.

Steps to Conduct a CMA:

1. Select Comparables: Choose at least three similar properties in the same area.
2. Adjust for Differences: Make adjustments for any significant differences between the properties.
3. Analyze Data: Use the adjusted prices to estimate the value of the property in question.

Income Approach

This method is generally used for investment or commercial properties. It focuses on the net income the property is expected to generate.

Formula:

Property Value = Net Operating Income / Capitalization Rate

Cost Approach

This method calculates the cost to build a similar property from scratch, considering land value and depreciation. It's most useful for new buildings or specialized properties.

Steps:

1. **Estimate Land Value:** Determine the cost of the land as if it were vacant.
2. **Calculate Replacement Cost:** Estimate the cost of constructing a replica of the property.
3. **Account for Depreciation:** Subtract any depreciation from the replacement cost.

Financial Analysis

Cash Flow Analysis

For investment properties, understanding cash flow is crucial. Cash flow is the net income generated by the property after all expenses.

Cash Flow = Rental Income - (Operating Expenses + Mortgage Payments)

Return on Investment (ROI)

ROI measures the profitability of an investment and is expressed as a percentage.

Formula:

ROI = (Net Profit / Cost of Investment) × 100

Capitalization Rate (Cap Rate)

The cap rate is used to evaluate the potential profitability and risk of an investment property.

Formula:

Cap Rate = Net Operating Income / Current Market Value

Loan-to-Value Ratio (LTV)

LTV is a measure used by lenders to assess the risk associated with a mortgage loan.

Formula:

LTV = (Mortgage Amount / Appraised Value) × 100

Missouri-Specific Considerations

Property Taxes

Missouri has relatively low property taxes, but they can vary by location. Always consider the impact of property taxes on both valuation and financial analysis.

Market Trends

Local market trends can significantly impact property values. Factors like employment rates, interest rates, and economic growth should be considered.

Zoning Laws

Missouri has specific zoning laws that can affect property value. Always check the zoning requirements, especially for investment properties.

Advanced Valuation Techniques

Discounted Cash Flow (DCF)

This method is used for more complex investment properties and involves projecting the future cash flows and discounting them back to their present value.

Real Estate Pro Forma

A pro forma is a detailed financial model that includes all income and expenses and is often used for commercial properties.

Legal and Ethical Considerations

Appraisal Licensing

In Missouri, only licensed appraisers can conduct formal property valuations for federally-related transactions.

Ethical Guidelines

Agents must adhere to the National Association of Realtors (NAR) Code of Ethics, which requires providing honest and accurate information.

Conclusion

Understanding property valuation and financial analysis is crucial for anyone involved in real estate transactions in Missouri. These methods and financial metrics not only help in making informed decisions but also in negotiating better deals. Whether you're an aspiring homeowner, an investor, or a real estate professional, this chapter offers valuable insights into the complex but fascinating world of property valuation and financial analysis. Armed with this knowledge, you can navigate the Missouri real estate market with confidence and precision, ensuring that your transactions are both profitable and sound.

Mock Exam Property Valuation and Financial Analysis

➞1. Which property valuation method is most commonly used for residential properties?

    A. Sales Comparison Approach
    B. Cost Approach
    C. Income Approach
    D. ROI Method

Answer: A. Sales Comparison Approach
The Sales Comparison Approach is most commonly used for residential properties. It involves comparing the property to similar ones that have recently sold.

➞2. What does ROI stand for in real estate financial analysis?

    A. Return On Investment
    B. Rate Of Interest
    C. Real Estate Opportunity Index
    D. Return On Infrastructure

Answer: A. Return On Investment
ROI stands for Return On Investment. It's a key metric used to evaluate the profitability of an investment property.

➞3. What is the Debt Service Coverage Ratio (DSCR) used for?

    A. Calculating property taxes
    B. Assessing a property's ability to cover its debt obligations
    C. Determining the property's market value
    D. Calculating the monthly rent

Answer: B. Assessing a property's ability to cover its debt obligations

DSCR is used to assess a property's ability to cover its debt obligations. A DSCR greater than 1 indicates that the property is generating sufficient income to cover its debts.

➡ 4. Which of the following factors does NOT affect property valuation?

A. Location
B. Size and Layout
C. Color of the walls
D. Market Conditions

Answer: C. Color of the walls

The color of the walls is generally not a significant factor affecting property valuation. Location, size, and market conditions are more impactful.

➡ 5. What is Cash Flow Analysis used for in real estate?

A. Calculating monthly income and expenses
B. Assessing property taxes
C. Determining market value
D. Calculating ROI

Answer: A. Calculating monthly income and expenses

Cash Flow Analysis is used to calculate the monthly income generated by the property, subtracting all expenses, to determine the net cash flow.

➡ 6. What does a DSCR of less than 1 indicate?

A. The property is generating sufficient income
B. The property is not generating enough income to cover debts
C. The property is overvalued
D. The property is undervalued

Answer: B. The property is not generating enough income to cover debts**

A DSCR of less than 1 indicates that the property is not generating sufficient income to cover its debt obligations.

➡ 7. In the Sales Comparison Approach, what is adjusted for when comparing properties?

  A. Only the size
  B. Only the location
  C. Features, location, and other factors
  D. Only the features

Answer: C. Features, location, and other factors

Explanation: In the Sales Comparison Approach, adjustments are made for differences in features, location, and other factors to make a fair comparison.

➡ 8. What is the Cost Approach commonly used for?

  A. Old properties
  B. New properties
  C. Commercial properties
  D. Rental properties

Answer: B. New properties

Explanation: The Cost Approach is often used for new properties. It involves calculating how much it would cost to replace the property, then adjusting for depreciation and land value.

➡ 9. Which of the following is NOT a financial analysis tool in real estate?

  A. ROI
  B. DSCR

C. Cash Flow Analysis
D. Gross Domestic Product (GDP)

Answer: D. Gross Domestic Product (GDP)
GDP is not a financial analysis tool used in real estate. ROI, DSCR, and Cash Flow Analysis are commonly used metrics.

10. What is the Income Approach commonly used for?

A. Residential properties
B. Commercial properties
C. New properties
D. Old properties

Answer: B. Commercial properties
The Income Approach is commonly used for commercial properties. It involves calculating the present value of future cash flows the property is expected to generate.

11. What does the term 'amortization' refer to in real estate?

A. The process of increasing property value
B. The gradual reduction of a loan balance through regular payments
C. The increase in property tax over time
D. The depreciation of property value due to age

Answer: B. The gradual reduction of a loan balance through regular payments
Amortization refers to the gradual reduction of a loan balance through regular payments over time.

12. What is the primary focus of a Comparative Market Analysis (CMA)?

A. To compare the ROI of different properties

B. To assess the fair market value of a property

C. To evaluate the debt service coverage ratio

D. To calculate the net operating income

Answer: B. To assess the fair market value of a property

A Comparative Market Analysis (CMA) is primarily used to assess the fair market value of a property by comparing it to similar properties that have recently sold or are currently on the market.

13. What does LTV stand for in real estate?

A. Loan To Value

B. Long Term Viability

C. Lease To Vendor

D. Land Transfer Value

Answer: A. Loan To Value

LTV stands for Loan To Value, which is a ratio that compares the amount of a loan to the value of the property being purchased.

14. What is the primary purpose of a cap rate in real estate?

A. To measure the risk associated with a property

B. To calculate the monthly mortgage payment

C. To determine the property tax rate

D. To assess the age of the property

Answer: A. To measure the risk associated with a property

The cap rate, or capitalization rate, is used to measure the risk associated with a property and its potential return on investment.

15. What is the formula for calculating Net Operating Income (NOI)?

A. Gross Income - Operating Expenses

B. Gross Income + Operating Expenses

C. (Gross Income - Operating Expenses) / Gross Income

D. Operating Expenses - Gross Income

Answer: A. Gross Income - Operating Expenses

Net Operating Income (NOI) is calculated by subtracting operating expenses from the gross income generated by the property.

16. What is the Debt Service Coverage Ratio (DSCR) primarily used for?

A. To determine the profitability of a property

B. To assess a borrower's ability to cover loan payments

C. To calculate property taxes

D. To evaluate the market value of a property

Answer: B. To assess a borrower's ability to cover loan payments

DSCR is used to evaluate a borrower's ability to cover loan payments from the property's net operating income.

17. What does the Gross Rent Multiplier (GRM) measure?

A. The property's operating expenses

B. The property's potential for appreciation

C. The property's value relative to its gross rental income

D. The property's maintenance costs

Answer: C. The property's value relative to its gross rental income

GRM measures the property's value in relation to its gross rental income.

18. What is the primary purpose of a 'due diligence' period in real estate transactions?

A. To secure financing
B. To conduct inspections and verify property details
C. To negotiate the price
D. To find tenants

Answer: B. To conduct inspections and verify property details
The due diligence period allows the buyer to conduct inspections and verify property details before finalizing the purchase.

19. What does the term 'equity' refer to in real estate?

A. The market value of a property
B. The difference between the property's market value and the outstanding loan amount
C. The annual rental income
D. The initial down payment

Answer: B. The difference between the property's market value and the outstanding loan amount
Equity is the difference between the market value of the property and the amount still owed on any loans.

20. What is a 'contingency' in a real estate contract?

A. A binding agreement
B. A penalty for late payment
C. A condition that must be met for the contract to proceed
D. An optional add-on to the contract

Answer: C. A condition that must be met for the contract to proceed
A contingency is a condition or action that must be met for a real estate contract to become binding.

⇒ 21. What is the primary advantage of a 'fixed-rate mortgage'?

　A. Lower initial payments
　B. Flexibility in payment amounts
　C. Interest rate remains constant
　D. No down payment required

Answer: C. Interest rate remains constant

The main advantage of a fixed-rate mortgage is that the interest rate remains constant over the life of the loan.

⇒ 22. What is the 'appraisal' primarily used for in real estate?

　A. To assess property taxes
　B. To determine the market value of a property
　C. To calculate the ROI
　D. To evaluate the property's condition

Answer: B. To determine the market value of a property

An appraisal is primarily used to determine the market value of a property, often for lending purposes.

⇒ 23. What does 'underwriting' refer to in the context of real estate financing?

　A. The process of verifying loan documents
　B. The process of evaluating a borrower's creditworthiness
　C. The drafting of the mortgage contract
　D. The calculation of interest rates

Answer: B. The process of evaluating a borrower's creditworthiness

Underwriting refers to the process where a lender evaluates the creditworthiness of a potential borrower.

24. What is 'cash flow' in the context of real estate investment?

A. The total value of the property
B. The money generated after all expenses are paid
C. The initial investment amount
D. The annual property tax

Answer: B. The money generated after all expenses are paid
Cash flow is the money left over after all expenses, including mortgage payments and maintenance, are paid.

25. What does 'closing costs' include in a real estate transaction?

A. Only the down payment
B. Only the broker's commission
C. Various fees like loan origination, appraisal, and legal fees
D. Only property taxes

Answer: C. Various fees like loan origination, appraisal, and legal fees
Closing costs include a variety of fees such as loan origination fees, appraisal fees, and legal fees, among others.

26. What is the primary purpose of a 'cap rate' in real estate investment?

A. To measure the risk associated with the property
B. To calculate the property taxes
C. To determine the mortgage interest rate
D. To assess the property's condition

Answer: A. To measure the risk associated with the property
The cap rate is used to measure the risk and potential return of a real estate investment.

27. What does 'amortization' refer to in a mortgage context?

A. The process of increasing property value
B. The process of paying off debt over time
C. The initial down payment
D. The annual property tax

Answer: B. The process of paying off debt over time

Amortization refers to the gradual reduction of a debt over a specified period.

28. What is a 'balloon mortgage'?

A. A mortgage with no down payment
B. A mortgage with a large final payment
C. A mortgage with fluctuating interest rates
D. A mortgage paid off in two years

Answer: B. A mortgage with a large final payment

A balloon mortgage requires a large lump-sum payment at the end of the loan term.

29. What does 'leverage' mean in real estate investment?

A. Using borrowed funds for investment
B. Increasing the property's value through improvements
C. The ratio of debt to equity
D. The annual rental income

Answer: A. Using borrowed funds for investment

Leverage refers to the use of borrowed funds to finance a real estate investment.

30. What is 'escrow' in a real estate transaction?

A. A legal agreement between buyer and seller

B. An account where funds are held until the transaction is completed

C. The commission paid to the real estate agent

D. The initial offer made by the buyer

Answer: B. An account where funds are held until the transaction is completed

Escrow is an account where funds are held by a third party until specific conditions are met.

31. What is the 'loan-to-value ratio' used for?

A. To determine the interest rate

B. To calculate the down payment

C. To assess the risk of the loan

D. To measure property appreciation

Answer: C. To assess the risk of the loan

The loan-to-value ratio is used by lenders to evaluate the risk associated with a mortgage loan.

32. What does 'negative gearing' refer to in real estate investment?

A. When rental income exceeds expenses

B. When expenses exceed rental income

C. When the property value decreases

D. When the mortgage is paid off

Answer: B. When expenses exceed rental income

Negative gearing occurs when the costs of owning a property exceed the income it generates.

33. What is a '1031 exchange'?

A. A tax-deferred property exchange
B. A type of mortgage
C. A property valuation method
D. A type of property insurance

Answer: A. A tax-deferred property exchange

A 1031 exchange allows the owner to sell a property and reinvest the proceeds in a new property while deferring capital gains tax.

34. What is 'equity' in a property?

A. The market value of the property
B. The amount owed on the mortgage
C. The property's purchase price
D. The difference between the property's value and the mortgage balance

Answer: D. The difference between the property's value and the mortgage balance

Equity is the value of ownership interest in the property, calculated as the property's market value minus the remaining mortgage balance.

35. What does 'due diligence' mean in a real estate context?

A. The initial deposit made by the buyer
B. The research and analysis done before purchasing a property
C. The final inspection of the property
D. The negotiation process between buyer and seller

Answer: B. The research and analysis done before purchasing a property

Due diligence refers to the comprehensive appraisal and verification of a property before buying it.

36. What is a 'second mortgage'?

A. A mortgage taken out on a second property

B. A mortgage that replaces the first one

C. An additional loan secured by the same property

D. A mortgage with a second lender

Answer: C. An additional loan secured by the same property

A second mortgage is a loan that is secured by the equity in your home, in addition to your primary mortgage.

➡ **37. What is 'imputed rent'?**

A. Rent paid in advance

B. The rental value of a property you own and live in

C. Rent paid in installments

D. The tax on rental income

Answer: B. The rental value of a property you own and live in

Imputed rent is the economic theory of the rent you could be earning from leasing a property instead of living in it.

➡ **38. What is a 'fixed-rate mortgage'?**

A. A mortgage with fluctuating interest rates

B. A mortgage with a constant interest rate

C. A mortgage with a variable down payment

D. A mortgage that can be paid off at any time

Answer: B. A mortgage with a constant interest rate

A fixed-rate mortgage has an interest rate that remains the same for the entire term of the loan.

➡ **39. What is 'redlining'?**

A. A method of property valuation

B. Discriminatory practice in lending or insurance

C. A type of property insurance

D. A method of calculating mortgage interest

Answer: B. Discriminatory practice in lending or insurance

Redlining is an unethical practice where services are denied or priced differently in certain areas, often based on racial or ethnic composition.

➡ 40. What is 'gross yield' in real estate investment?

A. Annual rent divided by property value

B. Monthly rent multiplied by 12

C. Property value divided by annual rent

D. Annual rent minus expenses

Answer: A. Annual rent divided by property value

Gross yield is calculated by taking the annual rental income, dividing it by the property value, and then multiplying by 100 to get a percentage.

➡ 41. What does 'amortization' refer to in a mortgage context?

A. The process of increasing property value

B. The process of paying off debt over time

C. The process of calculating interest rates

D. The process of transferring property ownership

Answer: B. The process of paying off debt over time

Amortization refers to the gradual reduction of a debt over a given period.

➡ 42. What is a 'balloon payment'?

A. A small initial down payment

B. A large final payment at the end of a loan term

C. A monthly mortgage payment

D. An extra payment to reduce loan principal

Answer: B. A large final payment at the end of a loan term

A balloon payment is a large, lump-sum payment made at the end of a loan's term.

43. What is 'capital gains tax'?

A. Tax on rental income

B. Tax on the sale of a property

C. Tax on property purchase

D. Tax on mortgage interest

Answer: B. Tax on the sale of a property

Capital gains tax is levied on the profit made from selling a property.

44. What is a 'contingency' in a real estate contract?

A. A penalty clause

B. A condition that must be met for the contract to proceed

C. A fixed closing date

D. A mandatory down payment

Answer: B. A condition that must be met for the contract to proceed

A contingency is a condition or action that must be met for a real estate contract to become binding.

45. What is 'escrow'?

A. A type of mortgage

B. A legal arrangement where a third party holds assets

C. A method of property valuation

D. A type of property insurance

Answer: **B. A legal arrangement where a third party holds assets**

Escrow is a legal concept where a financial instrument or asset is held by a third party on behalf of two other parties in a transaction.

➡ 46. What is 'net operating income' in real estate?

A. Gross income minus expenses

B. Gross income plus expenses

C. Property value minus mortgage

D. Annual rent divided by property value

Answer: **A. Gross income minus expenses**

Net operating income is the total income generated by a property, minus the operating expenses.

➡ 47. What does 'underwriting' refer to in real estate?

A. The process of property valuation

B. The process of assessing the risk of a loan

C. The process of property inspection

D. The process of transferring property ownership

Answer: **B. The process of assessing the risk of a loan**

Underwriting is the process by which a lender evaluates the risk of offering a mortgage loan.

➡ 48. What is 'zoning' in real estate?

A. The process of property valuation
B. The division of land into areas for specific uses
C. The process of property inspection
D. The process of transferring property ownership

Answer: B. The division of land into areas for specific uses

Zoning refers to municipal or local laws or regulations that dictate how real property can and cannot be used in certain areas.

➛49. What is 'leverage' in real estate investment?

A. Using borrowed funds for investment
B. The ratio of debt to equity
C. The process of property valuation
D. The process of property inspection

Answer: A. Using borrowed funds for investment

Leverage in real estate refers to using borrowed capital for the purpose of expanding the potential return of an investment.

➛50. What is a 'real estate bubble'?

A. A period of rapid increase in property value
B. A period of rapid decrease in property value
C. A stable real estate market
D. A period of high rental income

Answer: A. A period of rapid increase in property value

A real estate bubble refers to a period of speculative excess where property prices rise rapidly and unsustainably.

Financing

Financing is a critical component of any real estate transaction. Whether you're a first-time homebuyer, a seasoned investor, or a real estate professional, understanding the nuances of financing can make a significant difference in the success of your real estate endeavors. This chapter aims to provide an in-depth look at the various financing options, terms, and strategies specific to the Missouri real estate market.

Types of Financing

Conventional Loans

These are mortgage loans not insured by a government agency and are the most common type of home loan.

- *Down Payment:* Usually 20%, but can be as low as 3%.
- *Credit Score:* Generally, a minimum of 620.

FHA Loans

Insured by the Federal Housing Administration, these loans are popular among first-time homebuyers.

- *Down Payment:* As low as 3.5%.
- *Credit Score:* Can be as low as 500, but with a higher down payment.

VA Loans

These are loans guaranteed by the Department of Veterans Affairs, available to veterans and active-duty military personnel.

- *Down Payment:* None required.
- *Credit Score:* Varies by lender, but usually, a minimum of 620 is needed.

USDA Loans

These loans are backed by the United States Department of Agriculture and are designed for rural properties.

- *Down Payment:* None required.
- *Credit Score:* Usually a minimum of 640.

Mortgage Terms

Interest Rates

- *Fixed-Rate Mortgage:* The interest rate remains the same throughout the loan term.
- *Adjustable-Rate Mortgage (ARM):* The interest rate can change at specific times.

Loan Term

- *15-Year Mortgage:* Higher monthly payments but less interest over the loan term.
- *30-Year Mortgage:* Lower monthly payments but more interest over the loan term.

Points

Points are fees paid to the lender at closing in exchange for a reduced interest rate.

Pre-Approval and Pre-Qualification

Pre-Qualification

A basic review of your financial information to give you an idea of the loan amount you might qualify for.

Pre-Approval

A more thorough verification process that includes a credit check and can provide you with a specific loan amount.

Missouri-Specific Financing Programs

First Place Loan Program

This Missouri-specific program offers first-time homebuyers lower interest rates and down payment assistance.

MHDC Loans

The Missouri Housing Development Commission offers various loan programs for low and moderate-income families.

Strategies for Financing

House Hacking

This involves buying a multi-unit property, living in one unit, and renting out the others.

Seller Financing

In this case, the seller acts as the lender. This can be beneficial if you can't qualify for a traditional loan.

Bridge Loans

These are short-term loans that help you buy a new home before selling your current one.

Tax Implications

Mortgage Interest Deduction

You can deduct the interest paid on your mortgage, which can offer significant tax savings.

Property Taxes

In Missouri, you can also deduct property taxes up to a certain limit.

Legal and Ethical Considerations

Truth in Lending Act (TILA)

This federal law requires lenders to disclose all terms of a loan clearly.

Missouri Secure and Fair Enforcement for Mortgage Licensing Act

This Missouri-specific law regulates mortgage brokers and lenders to protect consumers.

Conclusion

Financing is a complex but crucial aspect of real estate transactions. The options are numerous, and the terms can be intricate. However, with a solid understanding of the basics and the Missouri-specific programs and laws, you can navigate the financing landscape effectively. Whether you're looking to buy your first home, invest in a rental property, or help clients as a real estate professional, this chapter provides you with the tools you need to make informed and strategic financing decisions in the Missouri real estate market.

Mock Exam Financing

➡ 1. What is the minimum down payment generally required for a conventional loan?

A. 3.5%
B. 5%
C. 10%
D. 20%

Answer: D. 20%
Conventional loans usually require a higher down payment, often 20%, to avoid the need for mortgage insurance.

➡ 2. Which type of loan is backed by the Federal Housing Administration?

A. Conventional Loan
B. FHA Loan
C. VA Loan
D. ARM

Answer: B. FHA Loan
FHA loans are backed by the Federal Housing Administration and are designed for low-to-moderate-income borrowers.

➡ 3. Who is eligible for a VA loan?

A. First-time homebuyers
B. Veterans and active-duty military personnel
C. Low-income borrowers
D. Investors

Answer: B. Veterans and active-duty military personnel

VA loans are a benefit specifically for veterans and active-duty military personnel.

4. What is the main feature of an Adjustable-Rate Mortgage (ARM)?

A. Fixed interest rate
B. Lower initial interest rate
C. No down payment
D. Easier credit requirements

Answer: B. Lower initial interest rate

ARMs often start with lower rates than fixed-rate mortgages but the rates can increase over time.

5. What do interest-only loans allow you to pay initially?

A. Only the principal
B. Only the interest
C. Both principal and interest
D. Down payment only

Answer: B. Only the interest

Interest-only loans allow you to pay just the interest for a specific initial period, usually 5-10 years.

6. What is the first step in the mortgage process?

A. Loan Application
B. Pre-Approval
C. Underwriting
D. Closing

Answer: B. Pre-Approval

Before looking at properties, it's advisable to get pre-approved for a mortgage, which involves a lender checking your financial background.

7. What does the underwriting process involve?

A. Property inspection
B. Financial due diligence
C. Property selection
D. Loan repayment

Answer: B. Financial due diligence

During underwriting, the lender assesses your financial situation in detail and checks the property appraisal.

8. What is usually included in closing costs?

A. Monthly mortgage payments
B. Down payment
C. Loan origination fees
D. Property taxes

Answer: C. Loan origination fees

Closing costs can include loan origination fees, appraisal fees, title searches, and more.

9. What can significantly impact your monthly mortgage payments?

A. Type of property
B. Real estate agent's commission
C. Interest rates
D. Home inspection fees

Answer: C. Interest rates

The interest rate on your mortgage will significantly impact your monthly payments and the overall cost of the loan.

➡ 10. What is often included in monthly mortgage payments and paid by the lender annually?

   A. Closing costs
   B. Down payment
   C. Property taxes and homeowner's insurance
   D. Mortgage insurance

Answer: C. Property taxes and homeowner's insurance

Property taxes and homeowner's insurance are often included in monthly mortgage payments and are then paid by the lender on an annual basis.

➡ 11. What is the purpose of a good faith estimate?

   A. To provide an estimate of closing costs
   B. To lock in an interest rate
   C. To guarantee loan approval
   D. To assess property value

   Answer: A. To provide an estimate of closing costs

   A good faith estimate is provided by the lender to give you an idea of your closing costs.

➡ 12. What is a balloon mortgage?

   A. A mortgage with fluctuating interest rates
   B. A mortgage that requires a large payment at the end
   C. A mortgage with no down payment
   D. A mortgage with very low monthly payments

Answer: B. A mortgage that requires a large payment at the end

A balloon mortgage requires a large lump sum payment at the end of the loan term.

13. What does LTV stand for?

A. Loan To Value

B. Long Term Viability

C. Loan Transfer Variable

D. Low Transaction Volume

Answer: A. Loan To Value

LTV stands for Loan To Value, which is the ratio of the loan amount to the value of the property.

14. What is a home equity loan?

A. A loan for first-time homebuyers

B. A loan based on the value of your home

C. A loan for home repairs

D. A loan for investment properties

Answer: B. A loan based on the value of your home

A home equity loan is a type of loan where the borrower uses the equity of their home as collateral.

15. What is PMI?

A. Property Management Insurance

B. Private Mortgage Insurance

C. Public Mortgage Index

D. Property Maintenance Inclusion

Answer: B. Private Mortgage Insurance

PMI stands for **Private Mortgage Insurance**, which is usually required when the down payment is less than 20%.

16. What is a reverse mortgage?

A. A mortgage for seniors to convert equity into cash
B. A mortgage with reverse interest rates
C. A mortgage that pays the borrower
D. A mortgage for investment properties

Answer: A. A mortgage for seniors to convert equity into cash

A reverse mortgage allows seniors to convert the equity in their home into cash, usually for living expenses.

17. What is the main advantage of a 15-year mortgage over a 30-year mortgage?

A. Lower interest rates
B. Lower monthly payments
C. No down payment
D. No closing costs

Answer: A. Lower interest rates

A 15-year mortgage typically offers lower interest rates and allows you to build equity faster.

18. What does refinancing a mortgage mean?

A. Changing the terms of your mortgage
B. Extending your mortgage term
C. Taking out a second mortgage
D. Defaulting on your mortgage

Answer: A. Changing the terms of your mortgage

Refinancing involves replacing your existing mortgage with a new one, usually with better terms.

➡ 19. What is a credit score primarily used for in the mortgage process?

    A. To determine eligibility for certain types of loans
    B. To decide the size of the down payment
    C. To set the property value
    D. To calculate closing costs

Answer: A. To determine eligibility for certain types of loans

Your credit score is used to determine your eligibility for loans and the interest rate you'll receive.

➡ 20. What is a jumbo loan?

    A. A loan for small properties
    B. A loan exceeding conforming loan limits
    C. A loan for commercial properties
    D. A loan for mobile homes

Answer: B. A loan exceeding conforming loan limits

A jumbo loan is a mortgage that exceeds the conforming loan limits set by federal agencies.

➡ 21. What is the primary purpose of an escrow account in a mortgage?

    A. To hold the down payment
    B. To pay property taxes and insurance
    C. To cover repair costs
    D. To pay off the mortgage early

Answer: B. To pay property taxes and insurance

An escrow account is typically used to hold funds for paying property taxes and insurance.

22. What is an adjustable-rate mortgage (ARM)?

A. A mortgage with a fixed interest rate
B. A mortgage with an interest rate that can change
C. A mortgage with no interest
D. A mortgage for investment properties

Answer: B. A mortgage with an interest rate that can change

An adjustable-rate mortgage has an interest rate that can change periodically depending on market conditions.

23. What is the debt-to-income ratio?

A. The ratio of your monthly debt payments to your monthly income
B. The ratio of your loan amount to your property value
C. The ratio of your credit score to your income
D. The ratio of your down payment to your loan amount

Answer: A. The ratio of your monthly debt payments to your monthly income

The debt-to-income ratio is used by lenders to assess your ability to manage payments.

24. What is a pre-qualification in the mortgage process?

A. A binding agreement between you and the lender
B. An estimate of how much you can borrow
C. A guarantee of a loan
D. A final approval for a loan

Answer: B. An estimate of how much you can borrow

Pre-qualification is an initial step that gives you an estimate of how much you may be able to borrow.

25. What is the main disadvantage of an interest-only mortgage?

A. You can't pay off the principal
B. You pay more interest over time
C. You can't refinance
D. You need a large down payment

Answer: B. You pay more interest over time
With an interest-only mortgage, you end up paying more in interest because you're not reducing the principal.

26. What does APR stand for?

A. Annual Property Rate
B. Annual Percentage Rate
C. Approved Payment Rate
D. Average Price Range

Answer: B. Annual Percentage Rate
APR stands for Annual Percentage Rate, which includes the interest rate and other loan costs.

27. What is a conforming loan?

A. A loan that meets federal guidelines
B. A loan for investment properties
C. A loan with no down payment
D. A loan with a variable interest rate

Answer: A. A loan that meets federal guidelines

A conforming loan is one that adheres to the guidelines set by Fannie Mae and Freddie Mac.

➥ 28. What is a VA loan?

   A. A loan for veterans
   B. A loan for vacation homes
   C. A loan for very large properties
   D. A loan for agricultural properties

Answer: A. A loan for veterans

A VA loan is a mortgage loan in the United States guaranteed by the United States Department of Veterans Affairs.

➥ 29. What is the main advantage of a fixed-rate mortgage?

   A. Lower interest rates
   B. Interest rate can decrease
   C. Monthly payments stay the same
   D. No down payment required

Answer: C. Monthly payments stay the same

With a fixed-rate mortgage, your monthly payments are predictable because the interest rate stays the same.

➥ 30. What is underwriting in the context of mortgages?

   A. The process of verifying financial information
   B. The process of selling a mortgage
   C. The process of setting interest rates
   D. The process of inspecting a property

Answer: A. The process of verifying financial information

Underwriting involves verifying your financial information and assessing the risk of offering you a loan.

31. What is a balloon payment?

A. A small monthly payment
B. A large final payment
C. A payment made annually
D. A payment made bi-weekly

Answer: B. A large final payment

A balloon payment is a large, lump-sum payment made at the end of a loan term.

32. What is the purpose of private mortgage insurance (PMI)?

A. To protect the borrower from foreclosure
B. To protect the lender if the borrower defaults
C. To lower the interest rate
D. To eliminate the need for a down payment

Answer: B. To protect the lender if the borrower defaults

PMI is designed to protect the lender in case the borrower defaults on the loan.

33. What is the primary purpose of an amortization schedule?

A. To show the breakdown of each monthly payment into principal and interest
B. To show the total amount of interest paid over the life of the loan
C. To show the property's appreciation value over time
D. To show the borrower's credit score

Answer: A. To show the breakdown of each monthly payment into principal and interest

An amortization schedule provides a detailed breakdown of each monthly payment, showing how much goes toward the principal and how much goes toward interest.

➡ 34. What is a fixed-rate mortgage?

A. A mortgage with an interest rate that changes over time
B. A mortgage with a constant interest rate for the life of the loan
C. A mortgage with varying monthly payments
D. A mortgage with no interest

Answer: B. A mortgage with a constant interest rate for the life of the loan

A fixed-rate mortgage has an interest rate that remains the same for the entire term of the loan, providing predictability in payments.

➡ 35. What is a home equity line of credit (HELOC)?

A. A fixed-rate loan
B. A revolving line of credit
C. A type of insurance
D. A government grant

Answer: B. A revolving line of credit

A HELOC is a revolving line of credit that uses your home as collateral.

➡ 36. What is the loan-to-value ratio (LTV)?

A. The ratio of the loan amount to the property value
B. The ratio of the down payment to the loan amount
C. The ratio of the interest rate to the loan amount
D. The ratio of the loan amount to the borrower's income

Answer: A. The ratio of the loan amount to the property value

The loan-to-value ratio is the amount of the loan compared to the value of the property.

37. What is a subprime mortgage?

A. A mortgage for borrowers with excellent credit
B. A mortgage for borrowers with poor credit
C. A mortgage with no interest
D. A mortgage for commercial properties

Answer: B. A mortgage for borrowers with poor credit

A subprime mortgage is designed for borrowers who have poor credit history.

38. What is refinancing?

A. Taking out a second mortgage
B. Replacing an existing loan with a new one
C. Changing the terms of your existing loan
D. Selling your mortgage to another lender

Answer: B. Replacing an existing loan with a new one

Refinancing involves replacing an existing loan with a new one, usually with better terms.

39. What is a bridge loan?

A. A loan for construction projects
B. A short-term loan to cover the period between two long-term loans
C. A loan for first-time homebuyers
D. A loan for renovating a property

Answer: B. A short-term loan to cover the period between two long-term loans

A bridge loan is a short-term loan used until a person secures permanent financing.

➡ 40. What is a seller carry-back?

A. When the seller pays the closing costs
B. When the seller acts as the lender
C. When the seller pays for repairs
D. When the seller pays the agent's commission

Answer: B. When the seller acts as the lender
In a seller carry-back, the seller provides financing to the buyer, essentially acting as the lender.

➡ 41. What is the Loan-to-Value (LTV) ratio?

A. The ratio of the loan amount to the property's appraised value
B. The ratio of the loan amount to the borrower's income
C. The ratio of the property's appraised value to the market value
D. The ratio of the down payment to the loan amount

Answer: A. The ratio of the loan amount to the property's appraised value
The Loan-to-Value (LTV) ratio is calculated by dividing the loan amount by the property's appraised value.

➡ 42. What does a balloon payment refer to?

A. A large final payment at the end of a loan term
B. Monthly payments that gradually decrease
C. An initial down payment
D. Monthly payments that gradually increase

Answer: A. A large final payment at the end of a loan term
A balloon payment is a large, lump-sum payment made at the end of a loan's term.

➡ 43. What is the purpose of a "good faith estimate" in mortgage lending?

   A. To provide an estimate of closing costs
   B. To lock in an interest rate
   C. To assess the borrower's creditworthiness
   D. To determine the property's market value

Answer: A. To provide an estimate of closing costs
A "good faith estimate" is provided by the lender to give the borrower an estimate of the closing costs involved in the mortgage process.

➡ 44. What does the term "amortization" refer to in the context of a mortgage?

   A. The process of increasing the loan amount
   B. The process of paying off the loan over time
   C. The process of adjusting the interest rate
   D. The process of transferring the loan to another lender

Answer: B. The process of paying off the loan over time.
Amortization refers to the process of gradually paying off a loan over a specified period, usually through regular payments that cover both principal and interest.

➡ 45. What is the primary advantage of a fixed-rate mortgage over an adjustable-rate mortgage?

   A. Lower initial interest rate
   B. Interest rate can decrease over time
   C. Interest rate remains constant over the loan term
   D. Easier qualification criteria

Answer: C. Interest rate remains constant over the loan term

The primary advantage of a fixed-rate mortgage is that the interest rate remains constant over the term of the loan, providing predictability in payments.

46. What is private mortgage insurance (PMI)?

A. Insurance that protects the lender
B. Insurance that protects the borrower
C. Insurance that protects the property
D. Insurance that protects against natural disasters

Answer: A. Insurance that protects the lender

PMI is insurance that protects the lender in case the borrower defaults on the loan.

47. What is an escrow account primarily used for?

A. Investing in stocks
B. Paying property taxes and insurance
C. Saving for retirement
D. Paying off the mortgage early

Answer: B. Paying property taxes and insurance

An escrow account is typically used to pay property taxes and insurance premiums.

48. What is a debt-to-income ratio?

A. The ratio of a borrower's total debt to total income
B. The ratio of a borrower's credit score to income
C. The ratio of a borrower's assets to liabilities
D. The ratio of a borrower's monthly expenses to income

Answer: A. The ratio of a borrower's total debt to total income

The debt-to-income ratio is calculated by dividing a borrower's total debt by their total income.

49. What is the primary purpose of a rate lock?

A. To increase the interest rate over time
B. To decrease the interest rate over time
C. To secure an interest rate for a specified period
D. To allow the interest rate to fluctuate

Answer: C. To secure an interest rate for a specified period
A rate lock secures a specific interest rate for a set period, usually during the loan application process.

50. What is a pre-qualification?

A. A binding agreement between the lender and borrower
B. An initial assessment of a borrower's creditworthiness
C. A final approval for a loan
D. A legal document outlining the terms of the loan

Answer: B. An initial assessment of a borrower's creditworthiness
A pre-qualification is an initial evaluation of a borrower's creditworthiness, usually based on self-reported financial information.

Transfer of Property

The transfer of property is a pivotal stage in any real estate transaction. It involves various legal processes, documents, and professionals to ensure a smooth transition of ownership. This chapter aims to provide a comprehensive guide to the transfer of property in Missouri, covering everything from the initial contract to the closing process and beyond.

Types of Property Transfers

Sale and Purchase

The most common form of property transfer, involving a buyer and a seller.

Inheritance

Transfer of property upon the death of the owner, usually through a will or by intestate succession.

Gift

Property given voluntarily without payment in return.

Foreclosure

Transfer of property from a homeowner to a bank or lender due to default on a mortgage.

Key Documents in Property Transfer

Deed

The legal document that transfers ownership of the property. Types of deeds include:

- **_Warranty Deed:_** Guarantees that the seller owns the property free and clear.
- **_Quitclaim Deed:_** Transfers any ownership interest the seller has in the property without any guarantees.

Title Insurance

A policy that protects against any defects or issues with the title.

Bill of Sale

Lists any personal property included in the sale, such as appliances or furniture.

Closing Statement

A detailed account of all financial transactions involved in the sale.

The Role of Professionals

Real Estate Agents

They facilitate the transaction between the buyer and seller.

Title Companies

They conduct title searches and often host the closing.

Lawyers

They can provide legal advice and review contracts and deeds.

Notaries

They verify the identities of the parties signing the documents.

The Closing Process

Escrow

An account where all the funds are held until the closing is complete.

Final Walkthrough

The buyer inspects the property to ensure it's in the agreed-upon condition.

Closing Costs

Fees and expenses that are paid at the closing. These can include:

- Loan origination fees
- Appraisal fees
- Title search fees

Recording the Deed

After the closing, the deed is recorded in the public records, finalizing the transfer of property.

Missouri-Specific Regulations

Missouri Marketable Title Act

This law simplifies the title search process by limiting the examination period to 30 years.

Missouri Non-Resident Transfer Tax

Non-residents selling Missouri property may be subject to a withholding tax.

Missouri Condominium Law

Specific rules apply to the transfer of condominiums, including the right of first refusal for the condo association.

Common Issues and How to Avoid Them

Title Defects

Always get title insurance to protect against any title issues.

Property Liens

Ensure a title search is conducted to identify any liens on the property.

Contract Disputes

Always have a lawyer review contracts to ensure they are legally sound.

Post-Transfer Responsibilities

Property Taxes

The new owner is responsible for all future property taxes.

Utilities

Transfer all utility accounts into the new owner's name.

Home Insurance

Ensure you have adequate home insurance from the day of the closing.

Conclusion

The transfer of property is a complex but crucial part of the real estate process. It involves multiple parties, a variety of documents, and a series of legal procedures. However, with the right knowledge and preparation, you can navigate this process successfully. This chapter has aimed to provide a comprehensive guide to the transfer of property in Missouri, equipping you with the information you need to handle your next real estate transaction with confidence.

Mock Exam Transfer of Property

➡ 1. What is the most common form of voluntary property transfer?

   A. Foreclosure
   B. Eminent Domain
   C. Sales
   D. Adverse Possession

Answer: C. Sales
Sales are the most common form of voluntary property transfer, usually involving a straightforward transaction between a buyer and a seller.

➡ 2. Which type of deed offers the least protection to the buyer?

   A. General Warranty Deed
   B. Special Warranty Deed
   C. Quitclaim Deed
   D. Bargain and Sale Deed

Answer: C. Quitclaim Deed
Quitclaim Deeds offer the least protection as they come with no warranties.

➡ 3. What is the legal process by which a lender can take possession of a property due to default?

   A. Eminent Domain
   B. Foreclosure
   C. Adverse Possession
   D. Gifting

Answer: B. Foreclosure

Foreclosure is the legal process that allows a lender to take possession of a property when the owner defaults on mortgage payments.

4. What is the minimum requirement for a deed to be enforceable?

A. Oral Agreement
B. Written Instrument
C. Mutual Consent
D. Legal Capacity

Answer: B. Written Instrument

A deed must be in writing to be legally enforceable, complying with state laws.

5. What does a Preliminary Title Report outline?

A. Tax implications of the sale
B. Issues with the title
C. Financing options
D. Property valuation

Answer: B. Issues with the title

A Preliminary Title Report outlines any issues with the title that need to be resolved before the sale can proceed.

6. What is the purpose of opening an escrow account?

A. To hold funds and documents related to the transaction
B. To pay property taxes
C. To hold the seller's profit
D. To pay the real estate agent's commission

Answer: A. To hold funds and documents related to the transaction

An escrow account is opened to securely hold funds and documents related to the property transaction until all conditions are met.

⇒7. What is the term for gaining ownership of a property by occupying it for an extended period under certain conditions?

A. Eminent Domain
B. Foreclosure
C. Adverse Possession
D. Inheritance

Answer: C. Adverse Possession

Adverse Possession allows someone to gain ownership of a property by occupying it for an extended period, provided certain legal conditions are met.

⇒8. What type of deed only covers the period of the current owner's tenure?

A. General Warranty Deed
B. Special Warranty Deed
C. Quitclaim Deed
D. Bargain and Sale Deed

Answer: B. Special Warranty Deed

A Special Warranty Deed only covers the period of the current owner's tenure and does not extend back to the property's origins.

⇒9. What is the term for the government acquiring private property for public use?

A. Foreclosure
B. Eminent Domain
C. Adverse Possession

D. Gifting

Answer: B. Eminent Domain

Eminent Domain is the legal process by which the government can acquire private property for public use, provided they offer just compensation.

➡ 10. What is the most common form of consideration in property transfers?

A. Services
B. Money
C. Other assets
D. Promissory notes

Answer: B. Money

Money is the most common form of consideration in property transfers, although other assets or services can also serve this purpose.

➡ 11. What is the term for a legal claim against a property that must be paid off when the property is sold?

A. Lien
B. Mortgage
C. Easement
D. Covenant

Answer: A. Lien

A lien is a legal claim against a property that must be paid off when the property is sold.

➡ 12. What is the right to use someone else's land for a specific purpose called?

A. Easement
B. Lien

C. Covenant

D. Mortgage

Answer: A. Easement

An easement grants the right to use another person's land for a specific purpose.

➡ 13. What is the process of dividing a large parcel of land into smaller lots?

A. Zoning

B. Subdivision

C. Partitioning

D. Rezoning

Answer: B. Subdivision

Subdivision is the process of dividing a larger parcel of land into smaller lots.

➡ 14. What is the term for a restriction on how a property may be used?

A. Easement

B. Covenant

C. Lien

D. Mortgage

Answer: B. Covenant

A covenant is a restriction on how a property may be used, often found in property deeds or community bylaws.

➡ 15. What is the primary purpose of a title search?

A. To determine property value

B. To find any restrictions on the property

C. To discover any liens or encumbrances on the property

D. To assess the property's condition

Answer: C. To discover any liens or encumbrances on the property

The primary purpose of a title search is to discover any liens, encumbrances, or other issues that could affect the transfer of property.

➡16. What is the term for the transfer of property upon the owner's death without a will?

A. Probate
B. Intestate
C. Testamentary
D. Inheritance

Answer: B. Intestate

When a property owner dies without a will, the property is transferred according to intestate laws.

➡17. What is the term for a change in property ownership where the new owner assumes the mortgage?

A. Assumption
B. Novation
C. Subletting
D. Foreclosure

Answer: A. Assumption

Assumption is when a new owner takes over the existing mortgage of the property.

➡18. What is the term for the right of a government or its agent to expropriate private property for public use, with payment of compensation?

A. Eminent Domain

B. Foreclosure

C. Adverse Possession

D. Lien

Answer: A. Eminent Domain

Eminent Domain is the right of a government to expropriate private property for public use, with compensation.

➡ 19. What is the term for a written document that transfers title of property from one person to another?

A. Mortgage

B. Deed

C. Lien

D. Easement

Answer: B. Deed

A deed is a written document that transfers title of property from one person to another.

➡ 20. What is the term for a legal process that involves the distribution of a deceased person's property?

A. Probate

B. Intestate

C. Foreclosure

D. Eminent Domain

Answer: A. Probate

Probate is the legal process involving the distribution of a deceased person's property, especially if they died without a will.

▸ 21. What is the term for acquiring property through the unauthorized occupation of another's land?

A. Adverse Possession
B. Eminent Domain
C. Foreclosure
D. Probate

Answer: A. Adverse Possession

Adverse Possession is the process of acquiring property by occupying someone else's land without permission for a certain period of time.

▸ 22. What is the term for a legal document that confirms the sale of a property?

A. Bill of Sale
B. Deed of Trust
C. Title Certificate
D. Warranty Deed

Answer: A. Bill of Sale

A Bill of Sale is a legal document that confirms the sale and transfer of property from one party to another.

▸ 23. What is the term for a legal claim by a lender on the title of a property until a debt is paid off?

A. Mortgage
B. Lien
C. Easement
D. Covenant

Answer: A. Mortgage

A mortgage is a legal claim by a lender on the title of a property until the debt secured by the mortgage is paid off.

➡ 24. What is the term for the legal process by which a lender takes possession of a property due to non-payment?

A. Foreclosure
B. Eminent Domain
C. Probate
D. Adverse Possession

Answer: A. Foreclosure

Foreclosure is the legal process by which a lender takes possession of a property due to the borrower's failure to make required payments.

➡ 25. What is the term for a legal agreement that allows one party to use another's property for a specific purpose?

A. Lease
B. Mortgage
C. Easement
D. Lien

Answer: A. Lease

A lease is a legal agreement that allows one party to use another's property for a specific period and for a specific purpose.

➡ 26. What is the term for the official document that records the ownership of a property?

A. Title Certificate
B. Bill of Sale
C. Deed of Trust
D. Warranty Deed

Answer: A. Title Certificate

A Title Certificate is the official document that records the ownership of a property.

➡ 27. What is the term for a legal restriction on the use of land?

A. Zoning
B. Easement
C. Mortgage
D. Lien

Answer: A. Zoning

Zoning is a legal restriction that dictates how land in a certain area can be used.

➡ 28. What is the term for the right of a property owner to use and enjoy their property without interference?

A. Quiet Enjoyment
B. Eminent Domain
C. Probate
D. Foreclosure

Answer: A. Quiet Enjoyment

Quiet Enjoyment is the right of a property owner to use and enjoy their property without interference from others.

➡ 29. What is the term for a legal document that outlines the terms under which a loan will be repaid?

A. Promissory Note
B. Bill of Sale
C. Title Certificate
D. Warranty Deed

Answer: A. Promissory Note

A Promissory Note is a legal document that outlines the terms under which a loan will be repaid.

➡ 30. What is the term for the legal process of transferring property from a deceased person to their heirs?

A. Inheritance
B. Probate
C. Foreclosure
D. Eminent Domain

Answer: B. Probate

Probate is the legal process of transferring property from a deceased person to their heirs, especially if there is no will.

➡ 31. What is the term for the legal process that allows the government to take private property for public use?

A. Eminent Domain
B. Foreclosure
C. Adverse Possession
D. Probate

Answer: A. Eminent Domain

Eminent Domain is the legal process that allows the government to take private property for public use, usually with compensation to the owner.

➡ 32. What is the term for a legal agreement that secures a loan with real property?

A. Deed of Trust
B. Bill of Sale
C. Lease
D. Promissory Note

Answer: A. Deed of Trust

A Deed of Trust is a legal agreement that secures a loan with real property and serves as protection for the lender.

➡ 33. What is the term for the legal right to use a portion of another person's property for a specific purpose, such as a driveway or pathway?

A. Easement
B. Lien
C. Covenant
D. Right of Way

Answer: A. Easement

An easement is the legal right to use a portion of another person's property for a specific purpose, such as a driveway or pathway.

➡ 34. What is the term for a legal document that transfers ownership of property from the seller to the buyer?

A. Warranty Deed

B. Bill of Sale

C. Title Certificate

D. Promissory Note

Answer: A. Warranty Deed

A Warranty Deed is a legal document that transfers ownership of property from the seller to the buyer.

➡ 35. What is the term for the legal right to pass through someone else's land?

A. Right of Way

B. Easement

C. Zoning

D. Lien

Answer: A. Right of Way

Right of Way is the legal right to pass through someone else's land, often established through an easement.

➡ 36. What is the term for a legal document that outlines the terms of a rental agreement?

A. Lease Agreement

B. Bill of Sale

C. Deed of Trust

D. Promissory Note

Answer: A. Lease Agreement

A Lease Agreement is a legal document that outlines the terms of a rental agreement between a landlord and tenant.

➡ 37. What is the term for the legal process of verifying the validity of a will?

A. Probate

B. Eminent Domain

C. Foreclosure

D. Adverse Possession

Answer: A. Probate

Probate is the legal process of verifying the validity of a will and distributing the deceased's assets according to the will.

38. What is the term for a legal restriction placed on a property by a previous owner?

A. Covenant

B. Easement

C. Lien

D. Zoning

Answer: A. Covenant

A covenant is a legal restriction placed on a property by a previous owner, often outlined in the deed.

39. What is the term for the legal process of dividing a large parcel of land into smaller lots?

A. Subdivision

B. Zoning

C. Easement

D. Lien

Answer: A. Subdivision

Subdivision is the legal process of dividing a large parcel of land into smaller lots, often for the purpose of development.

➡ 40. What is the term for a legal document that grants someone the right to act on behalf of another in legal matters?

A. Power of Attorney
B. Lease Agreement
C. Deed of Trust
D. Promissory Note

Answer: A. Power of Attorney

Power of Attorney is a legal document that grants someone the right to act on behalf of another in legal matters.

➡ 41. What is the primary purpose of a deed restriction?

A. To limit the use of the property
B. To transfer ownership
C. To secure a loan
D. To establish easements

Answer: A. To limit the use of the property

Deed restrictions are used to limit the use of the property according to the terms set by the owner or the community.

➡ 42. What is the difference between a general warranty deed and a quitclaim deed?

A. A general warranty deed provides no warranties
B. A quitclaim deed provides full warranties
C. A general warranty deed provides full warranties
D. Both provide the same level of warranties

Answer: C. A general warranty deed provides full warranties

A general warranty deed provides the most protection to the buyer as it includes full warranties against any encumbrances.

43. What is the role of a title company in a property transaction?

A. Financing the purchase
B. Ensuring the title is clear
C. Conducting home inspections
D. Setting the property's price

Answer: B. Ensuring the title is clear

The title company ensures that the title to a piece of real estate is legitimate and then issues title insurance for that property.

44. What is the term for a written summary of a property's ownership history?

A. Title report
B. Chain of title
C. Deed of trust
D. Abstract of title

Answer: D. Abstract of title

An abstract of title is a written summary of a property's ownership history, which is used to determine the current status of the title.

45. What is the purpose of a gift deed?

A. To transfer property as a gift
B. To secure a mortgage
C. To lease the property
D. To sell the property

Answer: A. To transfer property as a gift

A gift deed is used to transfer property ownership without any exchange of money.

→46. What is a defeasible fee estate?

A. An estate that can be defeated or terminated
B. An estate that lasts forever
C. An estate that is free from encumbrances
D. An estate that is leased

Answer: A. An estate that can be defeated or terminated

A defeasible fee estate is a type of estate that can be defeated or terminated upon the occurrence of a specific event.

→47. What is the primary purpose of a deed?

A. To prove ownership of personal property
B. To transfer ownership of real property
C. To outline the terms of a mortgage
D. To establish a rental agreement

Answer: B. To transfer ownership of real property

The primary purpose of a deed is to transfer ownership of real property from one party to another. It serves as a legal document that shows the change in ownership.

→48. What is the primary purpose of a land contract?

A. To lease land
B. To sell land
C. To gift land
D. To mortgage land

Answer: B. To sell land

A land contract is primarily used to sell land, where the seller provides financing to the buyer.

49. What is the term for the right of the government to take private property for public use?

A. Eminent domain
B. Escheat
C. Foreclosure
D. Adverse possession

Answer: A. Eminent domain

Eminent domain is the right of the government to take private property for public use, with compensation to the owner.

50. What is the process of dividing a single property into smaller parcels?

A. Zoning
B. Subdivision
C. Partition
D. Condemnation

Answer: B. Subdivision

Subdivision is the process of dividing a single property into smaller parcels, often for the purpose of development.

Practice of Real Estate and Disclosures

The practice of real estate is a multifaceted profession that involves more than just buying and selling properties. It encompasses a wide range of activities, including marketing, negotiation, and most importantly, adhering to legal requirements such as disclosures. This chapter aims to provide an in-depth look into the practice of real estate in Missouri, focusing on the importance of disclosures and ethical considerations.

The Real Estate Practice Landscape

Brokerage Firms

Real estate agents often work under brokerage firms that provide the necessary support and resources. These firms are regulated by the Missouri Real Estate Commission.

Independent Agents

Some agents prefer to work independently, taking on the responsibilities of both the agent and the broker.

Teams

Real estate teams consist of multiple agents working together, often specializing in different aspects of real estate.

Niche Markets

Some agents specialize in specific types of real estate, such as commercial properties, luxury homes, or foreclosures.

Legal Obligations and Disclosures

Seller's Disclosure

In Missouri, sellers are required to provide a written disclosure statement that outlines the condition of the property. This includes any known defects or issues.

Lead-Based Paint Disclosure

For homes built before 1978, federal law requires sellers to disclose any known presence of lead-based paint.

Agency Disclosure

Agents are required to disclose whom they represent in a transaction, whether it's the buyer, the seller, or both.

Property Condition Disclosure

Agents must disclose any material facts they are aware of that could affect the property's value.

Dual Agency

In some cases, an agent may represent both the buyer and the seller. This must be disclosed and consented to by all parties.

Ethical Considerations

Fiduciary Duties

Agents have a fiduciary duty to their clients, meaning they must act in their best interests.

Fair Housing Act

Agents must adhere to the Fair Housing Act, which prohibits discrimination based on race, color, religion, sex, or national origin.

Confidentiality

Agents are obligated to keep their client's information confidential, even after the transaction has closed.

The Role of Technology

MLS (Multiple Listing Service)

A database where agents list properties for sale. It is a valuable tool for both agents and clients.

Virtual Tours

With advancements in technology, virtual tours have become increasingly popular, allowing potential buyers to view properties online.

Digital Signatures

Many transactions are now conducted digitally, including the signing of contracts and disclosures.

Marketing and Advertising

Traditional Methods

These include print ads, billboards, and open houses.

Digital Marketing

This includes social media advertising, email campaigns, and SEO (Search Engine Optimization).

Branding

Agents often create a personal brand to differentiate themselves in the market.

Continuing Education and Licensing

In Missouri, real estate agents are required to complete 12 hours of continuing education every two years to renew their license.

Common Pitfalls and How to Avoid Them

Misrepresentation

Always be truthful in your listings and disclosures to avoid legal repercussions.

Ignorance of the Law

Ignorance is not an excuse; always stay updated on real estate laws and regulations.

Poor Communication

Always keep lines of communication open with your clients to ensure a smooth transaction.

Conclusion

The practice of real estate in Missouri is a complex field that requires a deep understanding of both the market and the legal landscape. Disclosures play a crucial role in maintaining transparency and trust between all parties involved. By adhering to legal requirements and ethical standards, real estate professionals can ensure a successful and smooth transaction for their clients. This chapter has aimed to provide a comprehensive overview of the practice of real estate in Missouri, equipping you with the knowledge and tools you need to excel in this dynamic profession.

Mock Exam Practice of Real Estate and Disclosures

➡1. What is the primary focus of residential sales in real estate practice?

   A. Lease agreements
   B. Market trends
   C. Zoning laws
   D. Property management

Answer: B

Residential sales primarily focus on understanding market trends, property values, and the needs of clients.

➡2. What does a property manager NOT typically handle?

   A. Rent collection
   B. Maintenance and repairs
   C. Property appraisals
   D. Tenant relations

Answer: C

Property managers usually do not handle property appraisals; that's the job of a certified appraiser.

➡3. What is a material fact in real estate disclosures?

   A. The color of the walls
   B. The age of the roof
   C. The seller's reason for moving
   D. The brand of appliances in the home

Answer: B

Material facts include significant issues like the age of the roof, which could affect the property's value and condition.

4. What is the primary role of a leasing agent?

- **A.** Property valuation
- **B.** Finding tenants
- **C.** Handling legal actions
- **D.** Managing day-to-day operations

Answer: B

Leasing agents focus on finding tenants for vacant properties.

5. What must be disclosed about homes built before 1978?

- **A.** Asbestos
- **B.** Radon
- **C.** Lead-based paint
- **D.** All of the above

Answer: C

Federal law requires the disclosure of lead-based paint for homes built before 1978.

6. Who is responsible for providing a Seller's Property Disclosure?

- **A.** Buyer
- **B.** Seller
- **C.** Real estate agent
- **D.** Home inspector

Answer: B

The seller is responsible for filling out the Seller's Property Disclosure form.

7. What is NOT a type of disclosure in real estate?

A. Seller's Property Disclosure
B. Agency Disclosures
C. Financial Disclosures
D. Buyer's Property Disclosure

Answer: D

There is no such thing as a Buyer's Property Disclosure; the seller provides all necessary disclosures.

8. What does a real estate appraiser provide?

A. Legal advice
B. Estimated property value
C. Lease agreements
D. Tenant screening

Answer: B

Real estate appraisers provide an estimated value of a property.

9. What is included in natural hazards disclosures?

A. Property age
B. Utility availability
C. Flood risk
D. Previous owners

Answer: C

Natural hazards disclosures may include information on flood risk, earthquakes, and other natural disasters.

➡ 10. What is the primary ethical obligation of a real estate professional?

A. Maximizing profit
B. Acting in the best interests of their clients
C. Avoiding legal repercussions
D. Networking

Answer: B
Real estate professionals are ethically bound to act in the best interests of their clients.

➡ 11. What is the primary purpose of a Comparative Market Analysis (CMA)?

A. To determine property taxes
B. To set a listing price
C. To assess zoning laws
D. To evaluate mortgage options

Answer: B
A Comparative Market Analysis is primarily used to set a listing price for a property based on similar properties in the area.

➡ 12. What does the acronym RESPA stand for?

A. Real Estate Settlement Procedures Act
B. Residential Estate Sales Professional Association
C. Real Estate Service Providers Act
D. Residential Environmental Safety Protocol Act

Answer: A

RESPA stands for Real Estate Settlement Procedures Act, which regulates closing costs and settlement procedures.

13. What is the role of a fiduciary in real estate?

A. To provide financing
B. To act in the best interest of the client
C. To appraise the property
D. To market the property

Answer: B
A fiduciary is obligated to act in the best interest of the client.

14. What is NOT a common type of real estate fraud?

A. Property flipping
B. Equity skimming
C. False advertising
D. Open listing

Answer: D
Open listing is a type of listing agreement, not a form of real estate fraud.

15. What is the main purpose of a title search?

A. To find the property's market value
B. To verify the legal owner of the property
C. To assess the property's condition
D. To determine the property's zoning status

Answer: B
The main purpose of a title search is to verify the legal owner of the property.

16. What is a latent defect?

A. A defect that is visible during a walk-through
B. A defect that is hidden and not easily discoverable
C. A defect that has been repaired
D. A defect listed in the property disclosure

Answer: B

A latent defect is a hidden defect that is not easily discoverable during a routine inspection.

17. What is the primary purpose of a home inspection?

A. To assess the property's market value
B. To identify any defects or issues with the property
C. To verify the property's legal status
D. To finalize the mortgage terms

Answer: B

The primary purpose of a home inspection is to identify any defects or issues with the property.

18. What is a short sale?

A. A quick sale process
B. Selling the property for less than the mortgage owed
C. A sale with few contingencies
D. A sale where the buyer pays in cash

Answer: B

A short sale is when the property is sold for less than the amount owed on the mortgage.

19. What is earnest money?

A. The commission for the real estate agent
B. A deposit made by the buyer
C. The final payment at closing
D. Money paid for a home inspection

Answer: B

Earnest money is a deposit made by the buyer to show their serious intent to purchase the property.

20. What does a contingency in a real estate contract allow?

A. Immediate possession of the property
B. The buyer to back out under specific conditions
C. The seller to change the listing price
D. The real estate agent to collect a higher commission

Answer: B

A contingency allows the buyer to back out of the purchase under specific conditions without losing their earnest money.

21. What is the primary role of the Multiple Listing Service (MLS)?

A. To provide mortgage rates
B. To list properties for sale
C. To regulate real estate agents
D. To assess property taxes

Answer: B

The primary role of the MLS is to list properties for sale, making it easier for agents to find properties for their clients.

22. What is a dual agency?

A. When two agents represent the buyer

B. When one agent represents both the buyer and the seller

C. When two agents represent the seller

D. When an agent represents two buyers in the same transaction

Answer: B

Dual agency occurs when one agent represents both the buyer and the seller in a real estate transaction.

23. What is the main purpose of a seller's disclosure?

A. To list the price of the property

B. To disclose any known defects or issues with the property

C. To describe the property's features

D. To outline the commission rates

Answer: B

The main purpose of a seller's disclosure is to disclose any known defects or issues with the property.

24. What does the term "underwater mortgage" mean?

A. A mortgage with a high interest rate

B. A mortgage that is higher than the property's value

C. A mortgage for a property near a body of water

D. A mortgage that has been paid off

Answer: B

An underwater mortgage is when the remaining mortgage balance is higher than the current market value of the property.

25. What is a "pocket listing"?

A. A listing that is not yet on the market
B. A listing that is only shared with a select group of agents
C. A listing that has been sold
D. A listing that is under contract

Answer: B

A pocket listing is a listing that is not publicly advertised and is only shared with a select group of agents.

26. What is the main purpose of a buyer's agent?

A. To list properties for sale
B. To represent the buyer's interests
C. To conduct home inspections
D. To provide financing options

Answer: B

The main purpose of a buyer's agent is to represent the interests of the buyer in a real estate transaction.

27. What is a "balloon payment"?

A. A small monthly payment
B. A large final payment at the end of a mortgage term
C. A payment made halfway through the mortgage term
D. A payment made to the real estate agent

Answer: B

A balloon payment is a large final payment due at the end of a mortgage term.

28. What is "redlining"?

A. Drawing property boundaries

B. Discriminatory practice in lending or insurance

C. Highlighting important clauses in a contract

D. Marking properties that are under contract

Answer: B

Redlining is a discriminatory practice where services like lending or insurance are denied or priced higher for residents of certain areas.

29. What is the main purpose of an escrow account?

A. To hold the earnest money deposit

B. To pay the real estate agent's commission

C. To store the property's title

D. To hold funds for property taxes and insurance

Answer: D

The main purpose of an escrow account is to hold funds for property taxes and insurance.

30. What is a "contingent offer"?

A. An offer that is higher than the listing price

B. An offer that is dependent on certain conditions being met

C. An offer that has been accepted but not yet closed

D. An offer that is non-negotiable

Answer: B

A contingent offer is an offer that is dependent on certain conditions being met, such as financing or a satisfactory home inspection.

➡ 31. What is the primary role of a "listing agent"?

   A. To represent the buyer in a transaction

   B. To represent the seller in a transaction

   C. To conduct the home inspection

   D. To provide financing options

Answer: B

The primary role of a listing agent is to represent the seller in a real estate transaction, helping them to sell their property.

➡ 32. What is a "short sale"?

   A. A quick sale of a property

   B. Selling a property for less than the mortgage owed

   C. Selling a property without an agent

   D. A discounted sale for a quick closing

Answer: B

A short sale is when a property is sold for less than the amount owed on the mortgage.

➡ 33. What is "title insurance"?

   A. Insurance for property damage

   B. Insurance that protects against defects in the title

   C. Insurance for the mortgage lender

   D. Insurance for the real estate agent

Answer: B

Title insurance protects against defects in the title to the property.

➡ 34. What is "earnest money"?

A. Money paid to the real estate agent

B. Money paid to secure a contract

C. Money paid for a home inspection

D. Money paid for closing costs

Answer: B

Earnest money is a deposit made to a seller to show the buyer's good faith in a transaction.

35. What is a "FSBO" listing?

A. For Sale By Owner

B. For Sale By Operator

C. For Sale Before Offer

D. For Sale By Order

Answer: A

FSBO stands for "For Sale By Owner," indicating that the property is being sold without a real estate agent.

36. What is "amortization"?

A. The process of increasing property value

B. The process of paying off a loan over time

C. The process of transferring property

D. The process of evaluating a property's worth

Answer: B

Amortization is the process of paying off a loan over time through regular payments.

37. What is a "home warranty"?

A. A guarantee on the home's structure
B. A guarantee on the home's appliances and systems
C. A guarantee on the home's value
D. A guarantee on the home's location

Answer: B

A home warranty is a service contract that covers the repair or replacement of important home system components and appliances.

38. What is "zoning"?

A. The process of measuring a property
B. The division of land into areas for specific uses
C. The process of evaluating a property's value
D. The process of transferring property

Answer: B

Zoning is the division of land into areas designated for specific uses, such as residential, commercial, or industrial.

39. What is a "pre-approval letter"?

A. A letter confirming the property's value
B. A letter confirming mortgage eligibility
C. A letter confirming the property's condition
D. A letter confirming the real estate agent's credentials

Answer: B

A pre-approval letter is a letter from a lender indicating that a buyer is eligible for a mortgage up to a certain amount.

40. What is "escrow"?

A. A type of mortgage

B. A legal arrangement where a third party holds assets

C. A type of home inspection

D. A type of real estate contract

answer: B

Escrow is a legal arrangement in which a third party holds assets on behalf of the buyer and seller.

41. What is the purpose of a "Seller's Disclosure Statement"?

A. To disclose the seller's financial status

B. To disclose any known defects or issues with the property

C. To disclose the commission rate of the real estate agents

D. To disclose the buyer's financing options

Answer: B

The Seller's Disclosure Statement is used to disclose any known defects or issues with the property to potential buyers.

42. What does "dual agency" mean in real estate?

A. Two agents working for the same brokerage

B. An agent representing both the buyer and the seller

C. Two buyers competing for the same property

D. Two lenders involved in the financing

Answer: B

Dual agency occurs when a real estate agent represents both the buyer and the seller in the same transaction.

43. What is the primary purpose of a "title search"?

A. To find the property's market value
B. To check for any liens or encumbrances on the property
C. To assess the property's condition
D. To determine the zoning laws affecting the property

Answer: B

The primary purpose of a title search is to check for any liens or encumbrances on the property.

44. What does "FSBO" stand for?

A. For Sale By Owner
B. Full Service Brokerage Option
C. Fixed Selling Bonus Offer
D. Final Sale Before Offer

Answer: A

FSBO stands for "For Sale By Owner," indicating that the property is being sold directly by the owner without the representation of a real estate agent.

45. What is a "contingency" in a real estate contract?

A. A mandatory clause
B. A binding agreement
C. A condition that must be met for the contract to proceed
D. A non-negotiable term

Answer: C

A contingency is a condition that must be met for the contract to proceed.

46. What is the role of an "escrow agent"?

A. To market the property
B. To hold and disburse funds during a transaction
C. To negotiate the contract terms
D. To inspect the property

Answer: B

The role of an escrow agent is to hold and disburse funds during a real estate transaction.

47. What does "amortization" refer to?

A. The process of increasing property value
B. The process of paying off a loan over time
C. The process of transferring property ownership
D. The process of evaluating a property's worth

Answer: B

Amortization refers to the process of paying off a loan over time through regular payments.

48. What is the "right of first refusal" in a real estate context?

A. The right to refuse a home inspection
B. The right to be the first to make an offer on a property
C. The right to refuse to pay closing costs
D. The right to refuse to honor a contract

Answer: B

The right of first refusal gives a person the opportunity to be the first to make an offer on a property before the owner sells it to someone else.

49. What does "encumbrance" refer to in real estate?

A. A type of insurance policy
B. A claim or lien on a property
C. A type of mortgage loan
D. A legal restriction on property use

Answer: B

An encumbrance is a claim or lien on a property that affects its use or transfer.

50. What does "under contract" mean in real estate?

A. The property is being appraised
B. The property is available for sale
C. The property has an accepted offer but has not yet closed
D. The property is off the market

Answer: C

"Under contract" means that the property has an accepted offer but the sale has not yet closed.

Contracts

Contracts are the backbone of any real estate transaction. They provide the legal framework that outlines the rights, obligations, and expectations of each party involved. In Missouri, as in other states, real estate contracts must meet specific legal requirements to be enforceable. This chapter aims to provide a comprehensive guide to understanding contracts in the context of Missouri real estate, from the basic elements to the various types of contracts you'll encounter.

The Essentials of a Valid Contract

Offer and Acceptance

A contract begins with an offer from one party and acceptance from another. Both must be clear and unequivocal for the contract to be valid.

Consideration

This is something of value exchanged between parties. In real estate, this is often the property and the money exchanged for it.

Legal Purpose

The contract must be for a legal purpose. For example, a contract to sell a stolen property would be invalid.

Competent Parties

Both parties must be of sound mind, not under the influence of substances, and of legal age to enter into a contract.

Mutual Assent

Both parties must understand and agree to the terms of the contract.

Types of Real Estate Contracts

Purchase Agreement

This is the most common type of contract, outlining the terms and conditions under which a property will be sold.

Lease Agreement

This contract outlines the terms under which one party agrees to rent property owned by another party.

Listing Agreement

This is a contract between a seller and a real estate agent, outlining the terms under which the agent will sell the property.

Buyer's Agency Agreement

This contract outlines the relationship between a buyer and a real estate agent.

Land Contract

Also known as a "contract for deed," this agreement allows the buyer to use the property while making payments but doesn't transfer legal ownership until the full price is paid.

Missouri-Specific Provisions

Earnest Money Deposit

In Missouri, it's common for the buyer to provide an earnest money deposit as a show of good faith.

Contingencies

Missouri law allows for various contingencies, such as financing or inspection contingencies, that must be met for the contract to proceed.

Disclosure Requirements

Missouri has specific disclosure requirements, such as the need for a seller to provide a written disclosure statement about the condition of the property.

Closing Costs

The contract should specify who will pay for what at closing, which can be negotiated between the buyer and seller.

Contract Termination

Breach of Contract

If one party fails to fulfill their obligations, the other may have the right to terminate the contract.

Mutual Agreement

Both parties can agree to terminate the contract under mutually agreed-upon terms.

Contingency Clauses

If certain conditions are not met, a party may have the right to terminate the contract.

Ethical and Legal Considerations

Full Disclosure

Both parties should disclose all material facts. Failure to do so could result in legal consequences.

Fair Representation

Agents must fairly and accurately represent the property and the terms of the contract.

Compliance with Laws

All contracts must comply with federal, state, and local laws, including fair housing laws and anti-discrimination statutes.

Technology and Contracts

Electronic Signatures

Missouri law recognizes electronic signatures, making it easier to execute contracts remotely.

Digital Storage

Contracts and related documents can be stored digitally, but make sure they are secure to protect sensitive information.

Conclusion

Contracts are a critical component in the practice of real estate in Missouri. They provide the legal scaffolding that supports the complex process of buying, selling, or leasing property. Understanding the intricacies of real estate contracts, from the basic elements required for validity to the specific types of contracts you'll encounter, is crucial for anyone involved in a real estate transaction. This chapter has aimed to equip you with the knowledge you need to navigate contracts effectively, ensuring that you're well-prepared for any challenges that may arise.

Mock Exam Contracts

1. What is the primary purpose of a Purchase Agreement in real estate?

A. To outline the commission for the real estate agent
B. To set the stage for the relationship between buyer and seller
C. To provide a warranty for the property
D. To list the property on MLS

Answer: B

The Purchase Agreement serves as the cornerstone of any real estate transaction, outlining the terms and conditions between the buyer and seller.

2. Which type of lease requires the tenant to pay a flat rent while the landlord pays for all property charges?

A. Gross Lease
B. Net Lease
C. Triple Net Lease
D. Modified Gross Lease

Answer: A

In a Gross Lease, the tenant pays a flat rent and the landlord is responsible for all property charges.

3. What is "Consideration" in a contract?

A. A thoughtful gesture
B. Money or something of value exchanged
C. A legal requirement
D. A counteroffer

Answer: B

Consideration refers to something of value that is exchanged between parties in a contract. It can be money, services, or even a promise.

4. What happens in a Material Breach of contract?

A. A minor failure in performance
B. A significant failure in performance
C. A legal dispute
D. Contract is automatically renewed

Answer: B

A Material Breach is a significant failure in performance that allows the other party to seek remedies.

5. Which clause in a contract specifies what will happen if issues are found during an inspection?

A. Contingency Clause
B. Disclosure Clause
C. Inspection Clause
D. Arbitration Clause

Answer: C

The Inspection Clause outlines the type of inspection, who will conduct it, and what actions will be taken if issues are found.

6. What does a "Straight Option" in an Option Agreement provide?

A. The right to lease the property
B. The exclusive right to purchase within a certain time
C. The right to sublease the property

D. The right to first refusal

Answer: B

A Straight Option gives the buyer the exclusive right to purchase the property within a specified time frame.

➡ 7. Who cannot legally enter into a contract?

A. A licensed real estate agent
B. A minor
C. A property manager
D. A real estate investor

Answer: B

Minors are not legally competent to enter into contracts.

➡ 8. What is the primary purpose of Disclosure Clauses?

A. To outline the commission structure
B. To state federal and state requirements for property disclosure
C. To specify the type of inspection
D. To set the rent amount in a lease

Answer: B

Disclosure Clauses are used to state federal and state requirements for property disclosure, such as the presence of lead paint.

➡ 9. What is a Conditional Sale Agreement?

A. The property is sold as-is
B. The sale is conditional upon certain criteria
C. The buyer has the option to purchase later

D. The seller can back out at any time

Answer: B

A Conditional Sale Agreement means the sale is conditional upon certain criteria being met, such as the sale of the buyer's current home.

➡10. What is the legal status of a contract for illegal activities?

A. Valid
B. Null and void
C. Conditional
D. Binding

Answer: B

Contracts for illegal activities are considered null and void.

➡11. What is the role of an "Escrow Agent" in a real estate contract?

A. To market the property
B. To hold and disburse funds
C. To conduct inspections
D. To negotiate terms

Answer: B

The Escrow Agent holds and disburses funds according to the terms of the contract.

➡12. Which of the following is NOT a required element for a contract to be valid?

A. Offer and acceptance
B. Consideration
C. Legal purpose
D. Notarization

Answer: D

Notarization is not a required element for a contract to be valid.

➡ 13. What is the "Statute of Frauds" in relation to contracts?

A. A law that makes oral contracts illegal
B. A law that requires certain contracts to be in writing
C. A law that prevents fraudulent activities
D. A law that nullifies all previous contracts

Answer: B

The Statute of Frauds requires certain contracts, like those for real estate, to be in writing to be enforceable.

➡ 14. What does "Time is of the Essence" mean in a contract?

A. The contract has no expiration date
B. The contract must be executed within a specific timeframe
C. The contract can be modified at any time
D. The contract is not urgent

Answer: B

"Time is of the Essence" means that the contract must be executed within a specific timeframe, and delays could lead to penalties or termination of the contract.

➡ 15. What is a "Right of First Refusal"?

A. The right to reject any offer
B. The right to match or better any offer received by the seller
C. The right to be the first to view a property
D. The right to terminate a contract without penalty

Answer: B

The Right of First Refusal allows the holder to match or better any offer received by the seller before the property is sold to another party.

16. What is a "Contingent Contract"?

A. A contract that is dependent on certain conditions being met
B. A contract that is legally binding
C. A contract that has been terminated
D. A contract that is in the negotiation phase

Answer: A

A Contingent Contract is dependent on certain conditions being met, such as financing approval or a satisfactory home inspection.

17. What is "Specific Performance"?

A. A clause that specifies the responsibilities of each party
B. A legal remedy for breach of contract
C. A type of contract used in commercial real estate
D. A measure of a real estate agent's effectiveness

Answer: B

Specific Performance is a legal remedy that forces the breaching party to fulfill the terms of the contract.

18. What is the purpose of a "Hold Harmless Clause"?

A. To protect the buyer from market fluctuations
B. To protect one or both parties from liability for the actions of the other
C. To hold the property off the market for a specific period
D. To hold the buyer's deposit in escrow

Answer: B

A Hold Harmless Clause protects one or both parties from liability for the actions or negligence of the other party.

19. What is a "Bilateral Contract"?

A. A contract where only one party is obligated to perform
B. A contract where both parties are obligated to perform
C. A contract that is null and void
D. A contract that has been terminated

Answer: B

In a Bilateral Contract, both parties are obligated to perform their respective duties.

20. What is the "Implied Covenant of Good Faith and Fair Dealing"?

A. A written clause in every contract
B. An unwritten obligation for parties to act honestly and not cheat each other
C. A legal doctrine that makes all contracts public
D. A requirement for all contracts to be reviewed by a lawyer

Answer: B

The Implied Covenant of Good Faith and Fair Dealing is an unwritten obligation that requires parties to act honestly and not cheat or mislead each other.

21. What is a "Unilateral Contract"?

A. A contract where only one party is obligated to perform
B. A contract where both parties are obligated to perform
C. A contract that is null and void
D. A contract that has been terminated

Answer: A

In a Unilateral Contract, only one party is obligated to perform, while the other has the option but not the obligation to perform.

➡ 22. What is "Liquidated Damages"?

A. The actual damages suffered due to a breach
B. A pre-determined amount to be paid in case of a breach
C. The refundable part of a deposit
D. The non-refundable part of a deposit

Answer: B

Liquidated Damages are a pre-determined amount agreed upon by the parties to be paid in case of a breach of contract.

➡ 23. What is "Novation"?

A. The act of renewing a contract
B. The act of replacing one party in a contract with another
C. The act of nullifying a contract
D. The act of negotiating the terms of a contract

Answer: B

Novation is the act of replacing one party in a contract with another, effectively transferring the obligations to the new party.

➡ 24. What is an "Addendum"?

A. A change to the original contract
B. A separate agreement that is included with the original contract
C. A summary of the contract
D. A legal interpretation of the contract

Answer: B

An Addendum is a separate agreement that is included with the original contract to add or clarify terms.

25. What is "Recission"?

A. The act of renewing a contract
B. The act of terminating a contract and restoring parties to their original positions
C. The act of transferring a contract
D. The act of amending a contract

Answer: B

Recission is the act of terminating a contract and restoring the parties to their original positions, as if the contract had never existed.

26. What is "Parol Evidence"?

A. Written evidence
B. Oral evidence
C. Photographic evidence
D. Video evidence

Answer: B

Parol Evidence refers to oral statements or agreements that are not included in the written contract.

27. What is a "Counteroffer"?

A. An acceptance of the original offer
B. A rejection of the original offer
C. A new offer made in response to an original offer

D. A legal requirement for all contracts

Answer: C

A Counteroffer is a new offer made in response to an original offer, effectively rejecting the original offer.

➡ 28. What is "Earnest Money"?

A. Money paid to confirm a contract
B. Money paid to a real estate agent
C. Money held in escrow
D. Money paid for a home inspection

Answer: A

Earnest Money is money paid to confirm a contract, showing the buyer's serious intent to purchase.

➡ 29. What is "Force Majeure"?

A. A clause that frees both parties from liability in case of an extraordinary event
B. A clause that holds both parties liable regardless of circumstances
C. A clause that allows for price negotiation
D. A clause that requires a third-party mediator

Answer: A

Force Majeure is a clause that frees both parties from liability in case of an extraordinary event, like a natural disaster, that prevents one or both parties from fulfilling the contract.

➡ 30. What is "Severability"?

A. The ability to separate a contract into individual clauses
B. The ability to terminate a contract without penalty

C. The ability to transfer a contract to another party

D. The ability to amend a contract after signing

Answer: A

Severability is the ability to separate a contract into individual clauses, so that if one clause is found to be unenforceable, the rest of the contract remains in effect.

31. What does "Statute of Frauds" require for a real estate contract to be enforceable?

A. Verbal agreement

B. Written and signed agreement

C. Notarized agreement

D. Witnessed agreement

Answer: B

The Statute of Frauds requires that a real estate contract must be in writing and signed by the parties to be enforceable.

32. What is "Specific Performance"?

A. Monetary compensation for breach of contract

B. Forcing a party to carry out the terms of the contract

C. Nullifying the contract

D. Amending the contract

Answer: B

Specific Performance is a legal remedy that forces a party to carry out the terms of the contract as agreed.

33. What is "Time is of the Essence" in a contract?

A. A clause that allows for flexible deadlines

B. A clause that makes deadlines strictly binding

C. A clause that nullifies the contract after a certain time

D. A clause that allows for automatic renewal of the contract

Answer: B

"Time is of the Essence" is a clause that makes deadlines strictly binding, and failure to meet them could lead to breach of contract.

34. What is an "Open Listing"?

A. A listing agreement with multiple brokers

B. A listing agreement with one broker

C. A listing that is not publicly advertised

D. A listing that is only advertised within a brokerage

Answer: A

An Open Listing is a listing agreement where the seller can employ multiple brokers who can bring buyers to the property.

35. What is a "Net Listing"?

A. A listing where the broker's commission is a percentage of the sale price

B. A listing where the broker keeps all amounts above a certain price

C. A listing where the broker charges a flat fee

D. A listing where the broker's commission is paid by the buyer

Answer: B

In a Net Listing, the broker agrees to sell the owner's property for a set price, and anything above that price is kept as the broker's commission.

36. What is a "Contingency" in a contract?

A. A fixed term

B. A condition that must be met for the contract to be binding

C. A penalty for breach of contract

D. An optional term

Answer: B

A Contingency is a condition that must be met for the contract to proceed to closing.

37. What is "Due Diligence" in the context of a real estate contract?

A. The buyer's investigation of the property

B. The seller's disclosure of property defects

C. The broker's marketing efforts

D. The lender's appraisal of the property

Answer: A

Due Diligence refers to the buyer's investigation of the property to discover any issues that were not disclosed.

38. What is "Escrow"?

A. A legal process to resolve disputes

B. A third-party account where funds are held until conditions are met

C. A type of mortgage

D. A tax levied on property sales

Answer: B

Escrow is a third-party account where funds or assets are held until contractual conditions are met.

39. What is "Right of First Refusal"?

A. The right to be the first to purchase a property

B. The right to refuse any offer on a property

C. The right to terminate a contract

D. The right to amend a contract

Answer: A

Right of First Refusal gives a person the opportunity to be the first to purchase a property before the owner sells it to someone else.

40. What is "Joint Tenancy"?

A. Ownership by one individual

B. Ownership by two or more individuals with equal shares

C. Ownership by a corporation

D. Ownership by tenants

Answer: B

Joint Tenancy is a form of ownership where two or more individuals own property with equal shares and have the right of survivorship.

41. What is the primary purpose of a "Letter of Intent" in a real estate transaction?

A. To serve as a binding contract

B. To outline the terms under which a contract will be negotiated

C. To legally transfer property

D. To terminate an existing contract

Answer: B

A Letter of Intent serves to outline the terms under which the parties will negotiate a contract. It is generally not binding.

➡ 42. What does "Time is of the Essence" mean in a real estate contract?

A. The contract has an indefinite period
B. The contract must be executed within a specific timeframe
C. The contract can be terminated at any time
D. The contract is not time-sensitive

Answer: B

"Time is of the Essence" means that the contract must be executed within a specific timeframe, and failure to do so could result in penalties or termination of the contract.

➡ 43. What is the purpose of an "Addendum" in a real estate contract?

A. To correct a typo or error
B. To add additional terms or conditions
C. To terminate the contract
D. To renew the contract

Answer: B

An Addendum is used to add additional terms or conditions to an existing contract, effectively modifying it.

➡ 44. What is the effect of a "Waiver" in a contract?

A. It adds a new term to the contract
B. It removes a party's right to enforce a term of the contract
C. It extends the contract's duration
D. It makes the contract voidable

Answer: B

A waiver removes a party's right to enforce a particular term of the contract, essentially giving up that right.

45. What is "Specific Performance" in the context of a real estate contract?

A. Monetary compensation
B. Carrying out the exact terms of the contract
C. Termination of the contract
D. An optional performance

Answer: B

Specific Performance refers to carrying out the exact terms of the contract, usually enforced through a court order.

46. What does "Novation" mean in a contract?

A. Renewal of the contract
B. Replacement of one party with another
C. Addition of a new term
D. Termination of the contract

Answer: B

Novation means the replacement of one party in the contract with another, effectively transferring the obligations to the new party.

47. What does "Force Majeure" refer to in a contract?

A. A type of fraud
B. An act of God or unforeseen circumstances
C. A breach of contract
D. A type of contingency

Answer: B

Force Majeure refers to unforeseen circumstances or "acts of God" that prevent one or both parties from fulfilling the contract. It usually allows for the contract to be terminated or suspended.

48. What is the role of an "Escrow Agent"?

A. To negotiate the contract
B. To hold and disburse funds or documents
C. To enforce the contract
D. To terminate the contract

Answer: B

An Escrow Agent holds and disburses funds or documents as per the terms of the contract.

49. What is "Right of First Refusal" in a real estate contract?

A. The right to back out of the contract first
B. The right to match any offer received by the seller
C. The right to inspect the property first
D. The right to make the first offer on a property

Answer: B

Right of First Refusal gives a party the right to match any offer received by the seller, usually before the property is sold to another buyer.

50. What is "Earnest Money" in the context of a real estate contract?

A. The commission for the real estate agent
B. A deposit made by the buyer to show good faith
C. The final payment made at closing
D. A refundable deposit

Answer: B

Earnest Money is a deposit made by the buyer to show good faith and secure the contract. It is usually non-refundable and is applied to the purchase price.

Real Estate Calculations

Real estate calculations are an integral part of the real estate industry. Whether you're an agent, a buyer, or an investor, understanding the numbers is crucial. This chapter will delve into the most important calculations you'll encounter, from mortgage payments to investment returns.

Property Valuation

- Comparative Market Analysis (CMA)

A Comparative Market Analysis (CMA) is the cornerstone of property valuation. It involves comparing the property in question to similar properties ("comparables" or "comps") that have recently sold in the area.

Formula:

Property Value = Average Price of Comparable Properties x (1 + Adjustment Factor)}

Why It Matters:
Understanding how to accurately perform a CMA can mean the difference between overpricing a property, causing it to sit on the market, or underpricing it and losing money.

- Capitalization Rate

The capitalization rate, or cap rate, is another essential metric for property valuation, particularly for income-generating properties.

Formula:

$$\text{Cap Rate} = \frac{\text{Net Operating Income}}{\text{Current Market Value}}$$

Why It Matters:

The cap rate gives you a quick way to compare the profitability of different investment properties.

Financing Calculations

- Mortgage Payments

Mortgage calculations are essential for both buyers and real estate professionals to understand.

Formula:

$$M = P \times \frac{r(1+r)^n}{(1+r)^n - 1}$$

Where :

M is the monthly payment,

P is the principal loan amount,

r is the monthly interest rate, and

n is the number of payments.

Why It Matters:

Knowing how to calculate mortgage payments allows you to assess the affordability of a property and helps in planning long-term finances.

- Loan-to-Value Ratio (LTV)

The Loan-to-Value ratio is a risk assessment metric that lenders use.

Formula:

$$\text{LTV} = \frac{Loan\ Amount}{Appraised\ Value} \times 100$$

Why It Matters:

A high LTV ratio might mean a riskier loan from a lender's perspective, potentially requiring the borrower to purchase mortgage insurance.

Investment Calculations

- Return on Investment (ROI)

ROI is a measure of the profitability of an investment.

Formula:

$$ROI = \frac{Net\ Profit}{Cost\ of\ Investment} \times 100$$

Why It Matters:

ROI gives you a snapshot of the investment's performance, helping you compare it against other investment opportunities.

- Cash-on-Cash Return

This metric gives you the annual return on your investment based on the cash flow and the amount of money you've invested.

Formula:

$$\text{Cash-on-Cash Return} = \frac{Annual\ Cash\ Flow}{Total\ Cash\ Invested} \times 100$$

Why It Matters:

Cash-on-cash return is crucial for understanding the cash income you're generating compared to the cash invested, providing a more accurate picture of an investment's performance.

Area and Volume Calculations

- Square Footage

Square footage is the measure of an area, and it's one of the most basic calculations in real estate.

Formula:

Area = Length x Width

Why It Matters:
Square footage affects everything from listing prices to renovation costs, so getting it right is crucial.

- Cubic Footage

Cubic footage is often used in commercial real estate to determine the volume of a space.

Formula:

Volume = Length x Width x Height

Why It Matters:
In commercial settings, cubic footage can be essential for understanding how a space can be used.

Prorations and Commissions

- Prorations

Prorations are used to divide property taxes, insurance premiums, or other costs between the buyer and seller.

Formula:

Proration Amount = $\frac{\text{Annual Cost}}{365}$ x Number of Days

Why It Matters:
Prorations ensure that both parties are only paying for their share of the costs during the time they own the property.

- Commission Calculation

Commissions are the lifeblood of most real estate agents and brokers.

Formula:

Commission = Sale Price x Commission Rate

Why It Matters:
Understanding how commissions are calculated can help agents set realistic business goals and expectations.

Conclusion

Mastering these calculations is not just a requirement for passing various real estate exams; it's a necessity for a successful career in real estate. This chapter has covered the essential calculations any real estate professional needs to understand.

Mock Exam Real Estate Calculations

1. What is the formula for calculating the Loan-to-Value ratio?

   A. Loan Amount / Appraised Value
   B. Appraised Value / Loan Amount
   C. Loan Amount × Appraised Value
   D. Appraised Value × Loan Amount

Answer: A

The Loan-to-Value ratio is calculated as Loan Amount divided by Appraised Value.

2. What does ROI stand for?

   A. Return On Investment
   B. Rate Of Interest
   C. Real Estate Opportunity
   D. Rate Of Inflation

Answer: A

ROI stands for Return On Investment, which measures the profitability of an investment.

3. What is the formula for calculating square footage?

   A. Length × Width
   B. Length × Height
   C. Length + Width
   D. Length / Width

Answer: A

Square footage is calculated by multiplying the length by the width of the area.

4. What is the formula for calculating mortgage payments?

A. $P \times (r(1+r)^n) / ((1+r)^n - 1)$
B. $P \times r \times n$
C. $P / r \times n$
D. $P \times n / r$

Answer: A

The formula for calculating mortgage payments is $P \times (r(1+r)^n) / ((1+r)^n - 1)$.

5. What is the formula for calculating the capitalization rate?

A. Net Operating Income / Current Market Value
B. Current Market Value / Net Operating Income
C. Net Operating Income × Current Market Value
D. Current Market Value × Net Operating Income

Answer: A

The capitalization rate is calculated as Net Operating Income divided by Current Market Value.

6. What does CMA stand for in real estate calculations?

A. Comparative Market Analysis
B. Capital Market Assessment
C. Current Market Appraisal
D. Comparative Monetary Assessment

Answer: A

CMA stands for Comparative Market Analysis, used for property valuation.

➡ 7. What is the formula for calculating Cash-on-Cash Return?

    A. Annual Cash Flow / Total Cash Invested × 100
    B. Total Cash Invested / Annual Cash Flow × 100
    C. Annual Cash Flow × Total Cash Invested
    D. Total Cash Invested × Annual Cash Flow

Answer: A

Cash-on-Cash Return is calculated as Annual Cash Flow divided by Total Cash Invested, multiplied by 100.

➡ 8. What is the formula for calculating prorations?

    A. Annual Cost / 365 × Number of Days
    B. Annual Cost × 365 / Number of Days
    C. Number of Days / Annual Cost × 365
    D. Number of Days × Annual Cost / 365

Answer: A

Prorations are calculated as Annual Cost divided by 365, multiplied by the Number of Days.

➡ 9. What is the formula for calculating cubic footage?

    A. Length × Width × Height
    B. Length × Width
    C. Length × Height
    D. Width × Height

Answer: A

Cubic footage is calculated by multiplying the length, width, and height of the space.

➡ 10. What is the formula for calculating commissions?

A. Sale Price × Commission Rate
B. Commission Rate × Sale Price
C. Sale Price / Commission Rate
D. Commission Rate / Sale Price

Answer: A

Commissions are calculated as Sale Price multiplied by Commission Rate.

➟11. What is the formula for calculating Gross Rent Multiplier (GRM)?

A. Property Price / Gross Annual Rents
B. Gross Annual Rents / Property Price
C. Property Price × Gross Annual Rents
D. Gross Annual Rents × Property Price

Answer: A

The Gross Rent Multiplier (GRM) is calculated by dividing the property price by the gross annual rents.

➟12. What is the formula for calculating depreciation?

A. (Cost of the Property - Salvage Value) / Useful Life
B. (Salvage Value - Cost of the Property) / Useful Life
C. Cost of the Property × Salvage Value
D. Salvage Value × Cost of the Property

Answer: A

Depreciation is calculated by subtracting the salvage value from the cost of the property and dividing by its useful life.

➟13. What does PITI stand for in mortgage calculations?

A. Principal, Interest, Taxes, Insurance

B. Payment, Interest, Taxes, Insurance

C. Principal, Income, Taxes, Insurance

D. Payment, Income, Taxes, Insurance

Answer: A

PITI stands for **Principal, Interest, Taxes, and Insurance**, which are the four components of a mortgage payment.

➡14. What is the formula for calculating equity?

A. Market Value - Mortgage Balance

B. Mortgage Balance - Market Value

C. Market Value × Mortgage Balance

D. Mortgage Balance × Market Value

Answer: A

Equity is calculated as the market value of the property minus the mortgage balance.

➡15. What is the formula for calculating net operating income (NOI)?

A. Gross Income - Operating Expenses

B. Operating Expenses - Gross Income

C. Gross Income × Operating Expenses

D. Operating Expenses × Gross Income

Answer: A

Net Operating Income (NOI) is calculated by subtracting operating expenses from gross income.

➡16. What is the formula for calculating the break-even point?

A. Fixed Costs / (Selling Price - Variable Costs)

B. (Selling Price - Variable Costs) / Fixed Costs
C. Fixed Costs × (Selling Price - Variable Costs)
D. (Selling Price - Variable Costs) × Fixed Costs

Answer: A

The break-even point is calculated by dividing fixed costs by the difference between the selling price and variable costs.

➡ 17. What is the formula for calculating the internal rate of return (IRR)?

A. NPV = 0
B. ROI = 100%
C. NPV × ROI
D. ROI × NPV

Answer: A

The internal rate of return (IRR) is the discount rate that makes the net present value (NPV) of all cash flows equal to zero.

➡ 18. What is the formula for calculating the price per square foot?

A. Total Price / Total Square Footage
B. Total Square Footage / Total Price
C. Total Price × Total Square Footage
D. Total Square Footage × Total Price

Answer: A.

The price per square foot is calculated by dividing the total price by the total square footage.

➡ 19. What is the formula for calculating the amortization schedule?

A. $P \times (r(1+r)^n) / ((1+r)^n - 1)$

B. P × r × n

C. P / r × n

D. P × n / r

Answer: A

The formula for calculating the amortization schedule is P × (r(1+r)^n) / ((1+r)^n-1).

➡ 20. What is the formula for calculating the future value of an investment?

A. P × (1 + r)^n

B. P × (1 - r)^n

C. P / (1 + r)^n

D. P / (1 - r)^n

Answer: A

The future value of an investment is calculated as P × (1 + r)^n.

➡ 21. How do you calculate the Net Operating Income (NOI) for a property?

A. Gross Income - Operating Expenses

B. Gross Income + Operating Expenses

C. Operating Expenses - Gross Income

D. Gross Income × Operating Expenses

Answer: A

Net Operating Income is calculated by subtracting the operating expenses from the gross income.

➡ 22. What is the formula for calculating the loan-to-value ratio (LTV)?

A. Mortgage Amount / Appraised Value

B. Appraised Value / Mortgage Amount

C. Mortgage Amount × Appraised Value

D. Appraised Value × Mortgage Amount

Answer: A

The loan-to-value ratio (LTV) is calculated by dividing the mortgage amount by the appraised value of the property.

➡ 23. What is the formula for calculating the cash-on-cash return?

A. Annual Pre-tax Cash Flow / Total Cash Invested

B. Total Cash Invested / Annual Pre-tax Cash Flow

C. Annual Pre-tax Cash Flow × Total Cash Invested

D. Total Cash Invested × Annual Pre-tax Cash Flow

Answer: A

The cash-on-cash return is calculated by dividing the annual pre-tax cash flow by the total cash invested.

➡ 24. What is the formula for calculating the debt service coverage ratio (DSCR)?

A. Net Operating Income / Debt Service

B. Debt Service / Net Operating Income

C. Net Operating Income × Debt Service

D. Debt Service × Net Operating Income

Answer: A

The debt service coverage ratio (DSCR) is calculated by dividing the net operating income by the debt service.

➡ 25. What is the formula for calculating the equity build-up rate?

A. (Principal Paid in Year 1 / Initial Investment) × 100

B. (Initial Investment / Principal Paid in Year 1) × 100

C. Principal Paid in Year 1 × Initial Investment

D. Initial Investment × Principal Paid in Year 1

Answer: A

The equity build-up rate is calculated by dividing the principal paid in the first year by the initial investment and then multiplying by 100.

26. What is the formula for calculating the gross operating income (GOI)?

A. Gross Potential Income - Vacancy and Credit Losses

B. Vacancy and Credit Losses - Gross Potential Income

C. Gross Potential Income × Vacancy and Credit Losses

D. Vacancy and Credit Losses × Gross Potential Income

Answer: A

The gross operating income (GOI) is calculated by subtracting vacancy and credit losses from the gross potential income.

27. What is the formula for calculating the effective gross income (EGI)?

A. Gross Operating Income + Other Income

B. Other Income - Gross Operating Income

C. Gross Operating Income × Other Income

D. Other Income × Gross Operating Income

Answer: A

The effective gross income (EGI) is calculated by adding other income to the gross operating income.

28. What is the formula for calculating the absorption rate?

A. Number of Units Sold / Number of Units Available
B. Number of Units Available / Number of Units Sold
C. Number of Units Sold × Number of Units Available
D. Number of Units Available × Number of Units Sold

Answer: A

The absorption rate is calculated by dividing the number of units sold by the number of units available.

➡ 29. What is the formula for calculating the price-to-rent ratio?

A. Home Price / Annual Rent
B. Annual Rent / Home Price
C. Home Price × Annual Rent
D. Annual Rent × Home Price

Answer: A

The price-to-rent ratio is calculated by dividing the home price by the annual rent.

➡ 30. What is the formula for calculating the yield?

A. Annual Income / Investment Cost
B. Investment Cost / Annual Income
C. Annual Income × Investment Cost
D. Investment Cost × Annual Income

Answer: A

The yield is calculated by dividing the annual income by the investment cost.

➡ 31. What is the formula for calculating the Gross Rent Multiplier (GRM)?

A. Sales Price / Monthly Rent

B. Monthly Rent / Sales Price

C. Sales Price × Monthly Rent

D. Monthly Rent × Sales Price

Answer: A

The Gross Rent Multiplier (GRM) is calculated by dividing the sales price by the monthly rent.

32. How do you calculate the Loan-to-Value ratio (LTV)?

A. Loan Amount / Appraised Value

B. Appraised Value / Loan Amount

C. Loan Amount × Appraised Value

D. Appraised Value × Loan Amount

Answer: A

The Loan-to-Value ratio (LTV) is calculated by dividing the loan amount by the appraised value of the property.

33. How do you calculate the Net Operating Income (NOI)?

A. Gross Operating Income - Operating Expenses

B. Operating Expenses - Gross Operating Income

C. Gross Operating Income × Operating Expenses

D. Operating Expenses × Gross Operating Income

Answer: A

The Net Operating Income (NOI) is calculated by subtracting the operating expenses from the gross operating income.

34. How do you calculate the Debt Service Coverage Ratio (DSCR)?

A. Net Operating Income / Debt Service
B. Debt Service / Net Operating Income
C. Net Operating Income × Debt Service
D. Debt Service × Net Operating Income

answer: A

The Debt Service Coverage Ratio (DSCR) is calculated by dividing the Net Operating Income by the Debt Service.

➡ 35. What is the formula for calculating the Break-Even Ratio (BER)?

A. (Operating Expenses + Debt Service) / Gross Operating Income
B. Gross Operating Income / (Operating Expenses + Debt Service)
C. (Operating Expenses + Debt Service) × Gross Operating Income
D. Gross Operating Income × (Operating Expenses + Debt Service)

Answer: A

The Break-Even Ratio (BER) is calculated by dividing the sum of operating expenses and debt service by the gross operating income.

➡ 36. How do you calculate the Effective Gross Income (EGI)?

A. Gross Income - Vacancy Losses + Other Income
B. Gross Income + Vacancy Losses - Other Income
C. Gross Income × Vacancy Losses + Other Income
D. Gross Income + Vacancy Losses × Other Income

Answer: A

The Effective Gross Income (EGI) is calculated by subtracting vacancy losses from the gross income and adding any other income.

➡ 37. What is the formula for calculating the Operating Expense Ratio (OER)?

A. Operating Expenses / Effective Gross Income

B. Effective Gross Income / Operating Expenses

C. Operating Expenses × Effective Gross Income

D. Effective Gross Income × Operating Expenses

Answer: A

The Operating Expense Ratio (OER) is calculated by dividing the operating expenses by the effective gross income.

38. How do you calculate the Cash-on-Cash Return?

A. Cash Flow Before Taxes / Initial Investment

B. Initial Investment / Cash Flow Before Taxes

C. Cash Flow Before Taxes × Initial Investment

D. Initial Investment × Cash Flow Before Taxes

Answer: A

The Cash-on-Cash Return is calculated by dividing the cash flow before taxes by the initial investment.

39. What is the formula for calculating the Amortization Factor?

A. Monthly Payment / Loan Amount

B. Loan Amount / Monthly Payment

C. Monthly Payment × Loan Amount

D. Loan Amount × Monthly Payment

Answer: A

The Amortization Factor is calculated by dividing the monthly payment by the loan amount.

40. How do you calculate the Equity Dividend Rate (EDR)?

A. Cash Flow After Taxes / Equity Investment

B. Equity Investment / Cash Flow After Taxes

C. Cash Flow After Taxes × Equity Investment

D. Equity Investment × Cash Flow After Taxes

41. What is the formula for calculating the Debt Service Coverage Ratio (DSCR)?

A. Net Operating Income / Debt Service

B. Debt Service / Net Operating Income

C. Net Operating Income × Debt Service

D. Debt Service - Net Operating Income

Answer: A

The Debt Service Coverage Ratio is calculated by dividing the Net Operating Income by the Debt Service.

42. How do you calculate the Gross Rent Multiplier (GRM)?

A. Property Price / Monthly Rent

B. Monthly Rent / Property Price

C. Annual Rent / Property Price

D. Property Price / Annual Rent

Answer: A

The Gross Rent Multiplier is calculated by dividing the property price by the monthly rent.

43. What is the formula for calculating Loan-to-Value ratio?

A. Loan Amount / Property Value

B. Property Value / Loan Amount

C. Loan Amount × Property Value

D. Property Value - Loan Amount

Answer: A

The Loan-to-Value ratio is calculated by dividing the loan amount by the property value.

44. How do you calculate the break-even point in a real estate investment?

A. Fixed Costs / (Selling Price - Variable Costs)
B. (Selling Price - Variable Costs) / Fixed Costs
C. Fixed Costs × Selling Price
D. Selling Price / Fixed Costs

Answer: A

The break-even point is calculated by dividing the fixed costs by the difference between the selling price and variable costs.

45. How do you calculate the Return on Investment (ROI) for a property?

A. (Net Profit / Investment Cost) × 100
B. (Investment Cost / Net Profit) × 100
C. Net Profit × Investment Cost
D. Investment Cost - Net Profit

Answer: A

The Return on Investment is calculated by dividing the net profit by the investment cost and then multiplying by 100.

46. How do you calculate the equity in a property?

A. Property Value - Mortgage Balance
B. Mortgage Balance - Property Value
C. Property Value × Mortgage Balance
D. Mortgage Balance / Property Value

Answer: A

Equity is calculated by subtracting the mortgage balance from the property value.

➡ 47. What is the formula for calculating the amortization payment?

A. Principal Amount / Number of Payments
B. Interest Rate / Number of Payments
C. (Principal Amount × Interest Rate) / Number of Payments
D. (Principal Amount × Interest Rate) / (1 - (1 + Interest Rate)^-Number of Payments)

Answer: D

The amortization payment is calculated using the formula mentioned.

➡ 48. What is the formula for calculating the Internal Rate of Return (IRR) for a real estate investment?

A. The discount rate that makes the Net Present Value zero
B. The rate that equals the Net Operating Income
C. The rate that equals the Debt Service
D. The rate that makes the Gross Income zero

Answer: A

The Internal Rate of Return is the discount rate that makes the Net Present Value of all cash flows from a particular investment equal to zero.

➡ 49. What is the formula for calculating the rate of return on an investment property?

A. (Net Profit / Cost of Investment) × 100
B. (Cost of Investment / Net Profit) × 100
C. Net Profit × Cost of Investment

D. Cost of Investment - Net Profit

Answer: A

The rate of return is calculated by dividing the net profit by the cost of the investment and then multiplying by 100.

50. How do you calculate the net profit from a real estate investment?

A. Selling Price - (Buying Price + Costs)
B. (Buying Price + Costs) - Selling Price
C. Selling Price × Buying Price
D. Buying Price / Selling Price

Answer: A

The Net Operating Income (NOI) is calculated by subtracting the operating expenses from the gross operating income.

Specialty Areas

The real estate industry is a vast and diverse field, offering a range of specialty areas that cater to various market segments and client needs. From residential to commercial, each specialty area requires a unique set of skills, knowledge, and expertise. This chapter aims to provide an in-depth look into the various specialty areas in Missouri real estate, helping you understand the nuances and opportunities each one presents.

Residential Real Estate

Single-Family Homes

The most common form of residential real estate, single-family homes are standalone structures that house one family. Agents must understand the local market, school districts, and community amenities.

Multi-Family Homes

These are structures like duplexes and triplexes that house more than one family. They are often considered a stepping stone to commercial real estate due to the complexities of managing multiple tenants.

Condominiums

Condos offer individual ownership within a larger building or community. Agents must be familiar with Homeowners Association (HOA) rules and fees.

Vacation Homes

Missouri, with its lakes and natural beauty, is a popular location for vacation homes. Agents should be knowledgeable about short-term rental regulations and seasonal market fluctuations.

Commercial Real Estate

Office Spaces

Agents specializing in office spaces must understand leasing terms, zoning laws, and the specific needs of businesses.

Retail Spaces

This involves properties like shopping centers, malls, and storefronts. Location and foot traffic are key factors.

Industrial Real Estate

This includes warehouses and manufacturing facilities. Agents need to understand industrial zoning laws and the logistical needs of businesses.

Agricultural Land

Missouri has a rich agricultural history. Agents must be familiar with soil types, water rights, and farming practices.

Investment Real Estate

Rental Properties

Investing in rental properties can provide a steady income. Agents should understand property management and tenant laws.

House Flipping

This involves buying a property, renovating it, and selling it for a profit. Agents must be skilled in estimating both costs and potential returns.

Real Estate Investment Trusts (REITs)

These are companies that own or finance income-producing real estate across various sectors. They offer a way to invest in real estate without owning physical property.

Niche Markets

Luxury Real Estate

This involves high-value homes and requires agents to have a network of affluent clients.

Historic Homes

Missouri has many historic homes that come with unique challenges, including preservation laws and specialized financing.

Foreclosures and Short Sales

These properties can be bought below market value but come with legal and financial complexities.

Technology in Specialty Areas

Virtual Tours

Especially useful in luxury and vacation home markets, virtual tours allow potential buyers to experience the property remotely.

Data Analytics

In investment real estate, data analytics tools can provide valuable insights into market trends and potential returns.

CRM Systems

Customer Relationship Management (CRM) systems are crucial for managing client relationships across all specialty areas.

Legal and Ethical Considerations

Fair Housing Laws

Regardless of the specialty area, agents must adhere to federal and state fair housing laws.

Disclosure

Full disclosure of any known issues with the property is legally required in all transactions.

Dual Agency

In some specialty areas like investment real estate, dual agency can present ethical challenges. Agents must be transparent and obtain written consent from both parties.

Conclusion

Specialty areas in Missouri real estate offer diverse opportunities for both agents and clients. Whether you're interested in residential, commercial, investment, or niche markets, understanding the unique requirements and challenges of each can help you make informed decisions and offer better services to your clients. This chapter aims to serve as a comprehensive guide, equipping you with the knowledge and insights you need to navigate the complex landscape of specialty areas in Missouri real estate.

Mock Exam Specialty Areas

1. Which type of real estate is often the entry point for many new agents and brokers?

A. Commercial
B. Industrial
C. Residential
D. Luxury

Answer: C. Residential

Explanation: The chapter states that residential real estate is often the entry point for many new agents and brokers.

2. What type of property is a penthouse?

A. Industrial
B. Commercial
C. Residential
D. Luxury

Answer: D. Luxury

Explanation: Penthouses are high-end apartments located on the top floors of high-rise buildings and fall under luxury real estate.

3. What is a key skill required in commercial real estate?

A. Financial Analysis
B. Knowledge of Industrial Machinery
C. Strong Interpersonal Skills
D. Discretion and Confidentiality

Answer: A. Financial Analysis

Explanation: Financial analysis is crucial in commercial real estate for understanding balance sheets, income statements, and cash flow.

➡4. What type of property is a factory?

A. Commercial
B. Industrial
C. Residential
D. Luxury

Answer: B. Industrial

Explanation: Factories are geared towards manufacturing, production, and distribution, which falls under industrial real estate.

➡5. What is a key regulatory aspect in industrial real estate?

A. Luxury tax implications
B. OSHA regulations
C. Fair Housing Laws
D. Commercial zoning laws

Answer: B. OSHA regulations

Explanation: Occupational Safety and Health Administration (OSHA) regulations are key in industrial real estate.

➡6. What type of property is a shopping mall?

A. Commercial
B. Industrial

C. Residential

D. Luxury

Answer: **A. Commercial**

Explanation: Shopping malls fall under commercial real estate as they are used for business activities.

➡ 7. **What is a key skill required in luxury real estate?**

A. Financial Analysis

B. Knowledge of Industrial Machinery

C. Strong Interpersonal Skills

D. Discretion and Confidentiality

Answer: **D. Discretion and Confidentiality**

Explanation: Clients in the luxury sector value their privacy highly, making discretion and confidentiality key skills.

➡ 8. **What type of property is a townhouse?**

A. Commercial

B. Industrial

C. Residential

D. Luxury

Answer: **C. Residential**

Explanation: Townhouses are multi-floor homes designed for individual or family living, which falls under residential real estate.

➡ 9. **What is a key regulatory aspect in residential real estate?**

A. Luxury tax implications

B. OSHA regulations

C. Fair Housing Laws

D. Commercial zoning laws

Answer: C. Fair Housing Laws

Explanation: Fair Housing Laws are key regulatory aspects in residential real estate to ensure equal opportunity in housing.

10. What type of property is a distribution center?

A. Commercial

B. Industrial

C. Residential

D. Luxury

Answer: B. Industrial

Explanation: Distribution centers are used for storing and distributing goods, which falls under industrial real estate.

11. What type of real estate involves the sale of businesses?

A. Commercial

B. Business Brokerage

C. Residential

D. Luxury

Answer: B. Business Brokerage

Explanation: Business Brokerage involves the sale of businesses, including their assets and real estate.

12. What is a key skill required in business brokerage?

A. Negotiation Skills

B. Knowledge of Industrial Machinery

C. Strong Interpersonal Skills

D. Financial Analysis

Answer: A. Negotiation Skills

Explanation: Negotiation skills are crucial in business brokerage to secure the best deals for clients.

13. What type of real estate involves the sale of farmland?

A. Commercial

B. Industrial

C. Agricultural

D. Luxury

Answer: C. Agricultural

Explanation: Agricultural real estate involves the sale of farmland and agricultural facilities.

14. What is a key regulatory aspect in agricultural real estate?

A. EPA Regulations

B. OSHA regulations

C. Fair Housing Laws

D. Luxury tax implications

Answer: A. EPA Regulations

Explanation: Environmental Protection Agency (EPA) regulations are key in agricultural real estate.

➡15. What type of property is a hotel?

A. Commercial

B. Industrial

C. Residential

D. Hospitality

Answer: D. Hospitality

Explanation: Hotels fall under hospitality real estate, which is a sub-category of commercial real estate.

➡16. What is a key skill required in hospitality real estate?

A. Customer Service

B. Knowledge of Industrial Machinery

C. Strong Interpersonal Skills

D. Financial Analysis

Answer: A. Customer Service

Explanation: Customer service is crucial in hospitality real estate to ensure guest satisfaction.

➡17. What type of real estate involves the sale of undeveloped land?

A. Commercial

B. Land

C. Residential

D. Luxury

Answer: B. Land

Explanation: The sale of undeveloped land falls under land real estate.

➡18. What is a key regulatory aspect in land real estate?

A. Zoning Laws
B. OSHA regulations
C. Fair Housing Laws
D. Luxury tax implications

Answer: A. Zoning Laws

Explanation: Zoning laws are key in land real estate to determine the types of development that can occur.

19. What type of property is a condominium?

A. Commercial
B. Industrial
C. Residential
D. Luxury

Answer: C. Residential

Explanation: Condominiums are multi-unit properties that are sold individually, which falls under residential real estate.

20. What is a key skill required in land real estate?

A. Negotiation Skills
B. Knowledge of Zoning Laws
C. Strong Interpersonal Skills
D. Financial Analysis

Answer: B. Knowledge of Zoning Laws

Explanation: Knowledge of zoning laws is crucial in land real estate to guide clients on permissible uses.

21. What is the primary focus of industrial real estate?

A. Warehouses
B. Hotels
C. Farmland
D. Condominiums

Answer: A. Warehouses

Explanation: Industrial real estate primarily focuses on warehouses and manufacturing buildings.

22. What is a 1031 exchange commonly used for?

A. Residential properties
B. Commercial properties
C. Agricultural properties
D. Industrial properties

Answer: B. Commercial properties

Explanation: A 1031 exchange is commonly used to defer capital gains tax in commercial real estate.

23. What is the main consideration in retail real estate?

A. Location
B. Size
C. Zoning
D. Tax implications

Answer: A. Location

Explanation: Location is the main consideration in retail real estate, as it directly impacts customer footfall.

24. What is the primary focus of residential real estate?

A. Single-family homes
B. Warehouses
C. Hotels
D. Farmland

Answer: A. Single-family homes

Explanation: Residential real estate primarily focuses on single-family homes, although it can include multi-family units.

25. What is the main consideration in luxury real estate?

A. Price
B. Location
C. Amenities
D. Size

Answer: C. Amenities

Explanation: Luxury real estate often focuses on the amenities offered, such as pools, gyms, and concierge services.

26. What is the primary advantage of investing in mixed-use real estate?

A. Diversification
B. Lower taxes
C. Easier management
D. Higher rent

Answer: A. Diversification

Explanation: Mixed-use real estate offers diversification as it combines residential, commercial, and sometimes industrial spaces.

➡27. What is the main disadvantage of investing in vacation real estate?

   A. Seasonal income
   B. High maintenance
   C. Zoning restrictions
   D. High taxes

Answer: **A. Seasonal income**

Explanation: Vacation real estate often has seasonal income, which can be a disadvantage for consistent cash flow.

➡28. What is the primary consideration when investing in student housing?

   A. Proximity to educational institutions
   B. Luxury amenities
   C. Tax benefits
   D. Size of the property

Answer: **A. Proximity to educational institutions**

Explanation: The primary consideration for student housing is its proximity to educational institutions.

➡29. What is the main benefit of investing in senior living communities?

   A. Lower maintenance
   B. Steady income
   C. Tax benefits
   D. High rent

Answer: **B. Steady income**

Explanation: Senior living communities often provide a steady income due to long-term leases.

⇒ 30. What is a triple net lease commonly used in?

A. Residential properties
B. Commercial properties
C. Industrial properties
D. Agricultural properties

Answer: B. Commercial properties

Explanation: A triple net lease is commonly used in commercial real estate, where the tenant pays property taxes, insurance, and maintenance costs.

⇒ 31. What is the primary focus of hospitality real estate?

A. Hotels and resorts
B. Warehouses
C. Office buildings
D. Farmland

Answer: A. Hotels and resorts

Explanation: Hospitality real estate primarily focuses on hotels, resorts, and other lodging options.

⇒ 32. What is the main consideration in agricultural real estate?

A. Soil quality
B. Location
C. Size
D. Zoning

Answer: A. Soil quality

Explanation: Soil quality is the main consideration in agricultural real estate for farming purposes.

33. What is the primary advantage of investing in REITs?

A. Liquidity

B. Control over property

C. Tax benefits

D. High rent

Answer: A. Liquidity

Explanation: REITs offer liquidity as they can be easily bought and sold on stock exchanges.

34. What is the main disadvantage of investing in office real estate?

A. High vacancy rates

B. Seasonal income

C. Zoning restrictions

D. High maintenance

Answer: A. High vacancy rates

Explanation: Office real estate can have high vacancy rates, especially in economic downturns.

35. What is the primary focus of mobile home parks?

A. Affordable housing

B. Luxury living

C. Commercial spaces

D. Agricultural land

Answer: A. Affordable housing

Explanation: Mobile home parks primarily focus on providing affordable housing options.

36. What is the primary consideration when investing in retail real estate?

A. Foot traffic

B. Tax benefits

C. Size of the property

D. Proximity to educational institutions

Answer: A. Foot traffic

Explanation: Foot traffic is crucial for the success of retail real estate.

37. What is the main benefit of investing in industrial real estate?

A. High rent

B. Long-term leases

C. Seasonal income

D. Tax benefits

Answer: B. Long-term leases

Explanation: Industrial real estate often comes with long-term leases, providing stable income.

38. What is a common disadvantage of investing in multi-family properties?

A. High maintenance costs

B. Low rent

C. Zoning restrictions

D. Seasonal income

Answer: A. High maintenance costs

Explanation: Multi-family properties often have higher maintenance costs due to multiple units.

39. What is the primary focus of medical real estate?

A. Hospitals and clinics
B. Office buildings
C. Warehouses
D. Hotels and resorts

Answer: **A. Hospitals and clinics**

Explanation: Medical real estate primarily focuses on hospitals, clinics, and other healthcare facilities.

40. What is the main consideration in raw land investment?

A. Zoning restrictions
B. Soil quality
C. Location
D. Size

Answer: **C. Location**

Explanation: Location is key in raw land investment for future development.

41. What is the primary advantage of investing in storage units?

A. Low maintenance
B. High rent
C. Tax benefits
D. Seasonal income

Answer: **A. Low maintenance**

Explanation: Storage units generally require low maintenance.

➡ 42. What is the main disadvantage of investing in co-working spaces?

A. High vacancy rates
B. Low rent
C. Zoning restrictions
D. Seasonal income

Answer: A. High vacancy rates

Explanation: Co-working spaces can have high vacancy rates, especially during economic downturns.

➡ 43. What is the primary focus of green real estate?

A. Energy efficiency
B. High rent
C. Tax benefits
D. Size of the property

Answer: A. Energy efficiency

Explanation: Green real estate primarily focuses on energy-efficient buildings.

➡ 44. What is the main benefit of investing in brownfield sites?

A. Tax incentives
B. High rent
C. Seasonal income
D. Long-term leases

Answer: A. Tax incentives

Explanation: Brownfield sites often come with tax incentives for redevelopment.

45. What is the primary consideration when investing in infill real estate?

A. Location
B. Size
C. Zoning restrictions
D. Soil quality

Answer: A. Location

Explanation: Infill real estate focuses on developing vacant or underused parcels within existing urban areas, so location is key.

46. What is the main disadvantage of investing in luxury real estate?

A. High maintenance costs
B. Seasonal income
C. Zoning restrictions
D. Low rent

Answer: A. High maintenance costs

Explanation: Luxury real estate often comes with high maintenance costs.

47. What is the primary focus of transit-oriented development?

A. Proximity to public transport
B. Luxury amenities
C. Tax benefits
D. Size of the property

Answer: A. Proximity to public transport

Explanation: Transit-oriented development focuses on properties close to public transport facilities.

48. What is the main benefit of investing in adaptive reuse properties?

A. Tax incentives
B. High rent
C. Seasonal income
D. Long-term leases

Answer: A. Tax incentives

Explanation: Adaptive reuse properties often come with tax incentives for redevelopment.

49. What is the primary consideration when investing in distressed properties?

A. Cost of renovation
B. Location
C. Size
D. Zoning

Answer: A. Cost of renovation

Explanation: The cost of renovation is a key consideration when investing in distressed properties.

50. What is the main disadvantage of investing in fixer-uppers?

A. High renovation costs
B. Low rent
C. Zoning restrictions
D. Seasonal income

Answer: A. High renovation costs

Explanation: Fixer-uppers often come with high renovation costs that can eat into profits.

Ethics and Legal Considerations

Navigating the complex world of real estate requires more than just market knowledge and negotiation skills. It also demands a strong ethical foundation and a thorough understanding of the legal landscape. This chapter delves into the ethical and legal considerations that are crucial for anyone involved in Missouri real estate.

Ethical Considerations

Code of Ethics

The National Association of Realtors (NAR) provides a Code of Ethics that serves as a guideline for real estate professionals. It covers duties to clients, the public, and other Realtors.

Fiduciary Duties

As a real estate agent, you owe your clients fiduciary duties, including loyalty, confidentiality, obedience, full disclosure, accounting, and reasonable care.

Dual Agency

Dual agency occurs when an agent represents both the buyer and the seller. This can lead to conflicts of interest and requires informed consent from all parties.

Misrepresentation and Fraud

Deliberately providing false information or concealing material facts is not only unethical but also illegal.

Fair Housing and Discrimination

Federal and state laws prohibit discrimination based on race, color, religion, sex, disability, familial status, or national origin.

Legal Considerations

Licensing Laws

In Missouri, real estate agents must be licensed by the Missouri Real Estate Commission. This involves passing an exam and fulfilling continuing education requirements.

Contract Law

Understanding the elements of a legally binding contract is essential. This includes offer, acceptance, consideration, legality of object, and contractual capacity.

Zoning and Land Use

Agents must be familiar with local zoning ordinances, which can affect property usage.

Environmental Laws

Missouri has specific laws regarding environmental hazards like lead-based paint and asbestos.

Property Rights and Ownership

Understanding the different types of property ownership, such as joint tenancy and tenancy in common, is crucial.

Intellectual Property

This includes the proper usage of photos and listings. Unauthorized use can lead to legal issues.

Legal Forms and Documents

Listing Agreements

This is a contract between a real estate broker and a seller.

Purchase Agreements

This outlines the terms and conditions under which a property will be sold.

Leases

For rental properties, a legally binding lease agreement is essential.

Disclosures

Missouri law requires the disclosure of material facts about a property's condition.

Risk Management

Errors and Omissions Insurance

This provides protection against legal claims for mistakes or negligence.

Record-Keeping

Maintaining accurate records is not only good practice but also a legal requirement.

Client Confidentiality

Protecting client information is both an ethical and legal obligation.

Technology and Legal Concerns

Electronic Signatures

Missouri law recognizes the legality of electronic signatures, but certain guidelines must be followed.

Data Protection

With the increasing use of technology, safeguarding client data is more important than ever.

Online Listings

Ensure that online listings are accurate and not misleading, as they are subject to the same legal standards as traditional listings.

Case Studies

Case 1: Fair Housing Violation

An agent in Missouri was found guilty of steering minority clients away from certain neighborhoods, a clear violation of Fair Housing laws.

Case 2: Breach of Fiduciary Duty

An agent representing both buyer and seller failed to disclose a termite problem, leading to legal repercussions.

Conclusion

Ethical and legal considerations are the backbone of a successful career in real estate. They protect the interests of both the agent and the client, ensuring a fair and transparent process for all parties involved. By adhering to ethical guidelines and staying informed about legal requirements, you can navigate the complexities of the Missouri real estate market with integrity and professionalism.

Mock Exam Ethics and Legal Considerations

1. What are the three main categories of the NAR Code of Ethics?

A. Duties to Clients, Duties to Realtors, Duties to the Public

B. Duties to Clients and Customers, Duties to the Public, Duties to Realtors

C. Duties to Sellers, Duties to Buyers, Duties to the Public

D. Duties to the Government, Duties to Clients, Duties to Realtors

Answer: B

The NAR Code of Ethics is divided into three main categories: Duties to Clients and Customers, Duties to the Public, and Duties to Realtors.

2. Which of the following is NOT a fiduciary duty?

A. Loyalty

B. Confidentiality

C. Manipulation

D. Full Disclosure

Answer: C

Manipulation is not a fiduciary duty. The fiduciary duties are loyalty, confidentiality, obedience, reasonable care, accounting, and full disclosure.

3. What is the primary purpose of zoning laws?

A. To increase property taxes

B. To regulate land use

C. To protect endangered species

D. To promote business

Answer: B

The primary purpose of zoning laws is to regulate land use, such as residential, commercial, or industrial zones.

4. What does 'reasonable care' in fiduciary duties imply?

A. Taking vacations regularly
B. Staying updated on market trends
C. Investing in real estate
D. Focusing on commission

Answer: B

'Reasonable care' means staying updated on market trends, legal changes, and other factors that could affect a client's decision.

5. What is the consequence of not adhering to full disclosure?

A. Increased commission
B. Legal repercussions
C. More clients
D. Promotion

Answer: B

Failing to adhere to full disclosure can lead to legal repercussions, including lawsuits and loss of license.

6. Which federal law is designed to ensure fair housing?

A. The Sherman Act
B. The Fair Housing Act
C. The Clayton Act
D. The Dodd-Frank Act

Answer: B

The Fair Housing Act is designed to prevent discrimination in housing based on race, color, religion, sex, or national origin.

➡ 7. What is the minimum age requirement for obtaining a real estate license in most states?

A. 16
B. 18
C. 21
D. 25

Answer: B

The minimum age requirement for obtaining a real estate license in most states is 18 years.

➡ 8. What is the key to resolving ethical dilemmas like dual agency?

A. Ignoring the issue
B. Full disclosure and informed consent
C. Choosing one party to represent
D. Consulting a lawyer

Answer: B

The key to resolving ethical dilemmas like dual agency lies in full disclosure and obtaining informed consent from all parties involved.

➡ 9. Which of the following is NOT an element that makes a contract legally binding?

A. Offer and acceptance

B. Consideration

C. Coercion

D. Legality of purpose

Answer: C

Coercion is not an element that makes a contract legally binding. A contract must have offer and acceptance, consideration, and legality of purpose to be legally binding.

10. What does the NAR Code of Ethics say about advertising?

A. It encourages aggressive advertising

B. It prohibits all forms of advertising

C. It requires truthful advertising

D. It promotes online advertising only

Answer: C

The NAR Code of Ethics requires that all advertising be truthful and not misleading.

11. What is the primary role of the Real Estate Commission in most states?

A. To sell properties

B. To regulate and license real estate agents

C. To build homes

D. To provide loans

Answer: B

The primary role of the Real Estate Commission in most states is to regulate and license real estate agents.

12. What is the statute of frauds?

A. A law that requires certain contracts to be in writing

B. A law that allows fraud in certain cases

C. A law that regulates online advertising

D. A law that deals with zoning issues

Answer: A

The statute of frauds is a law that requires certain contracts, like those for the sale of real estate, to be in writing to be enforceable.

13. What does RESPA stand for?

A. Real Estate Settlement Procedures Act

B. Real Estate Sales Professional Act

C. Residential Sales Property Act

D. Real Estate Security Policy Act

Answer: A

RESPA stands for Real Estate Settlement Procedures Act, which aims to provide transparency in the home buying process.

14. What is puffing in real estate terms?

A. Illegal misrepresentation

B. Exaggeration of property features

C. Accurate description of property

D. Undervaluing a property

Answer: B

Puffing refers to the exaggeration of property features, which is generally considered legal but can be ethically questionable.

15. What is the primary purpose of an escrow account?

A. To hold funds for investment

B. To hold funds until the completion of a real estate transaction

C. To pay for the agent's commission

D. To pay property taxes

Answer: B

The primary purpose of an escrow account is to hold funds until the completion of a real estate transaction.

16. What does the term "redlining" refer to?

A. Drawing property boundaries

B. Discriminatory lending practices

C. Marking properties for demolition

D. Highlighting important clauses in a contract

Answer: B

Redlining refers to discriminatory lending practices that deny loans or insurance to people based on their location, often targeting minority communities.

17. What is the difference between ethics and laws?

A. Ethics are legally binding, laws are not

B. Laws are legally binding, ethics are not

C. Ethics and laws are the same

D. Laws are optional, ethics are mandatory

Answer: B

Laws are legally binding rules that must be followed, while ethics are moral principles that guide behavior but are not legally enforceable.

18. What is the "doctrine of caveat emptor"?

A. Let the buyer beware
B. Let the seller beware
C. Buyer's premium
D. Seller's advantage

Answer: A

The doctrine of "caveat emptor" means "let the buyer beware," indicating that the buyer is responsible for due diligence.

19. What is a bilateral contract?

A. A contract with only one party
B. A contract with two parties
C. A contract with multiple parties
D. A contract that is not legally binding

Answer: B

A bilateral contract is a contract involving two parties where each party has made a promise to the other.

20. What is the role of a title company?

A. To market properties
B. To ensure the title is clear and prepare for its transfer
C. To provide loans
D. To build homes

Answer: B

The role of a title company is to ensure that the title to a piece of real estate is legitimate and to prepare for its transfer from the seller to the buyer.

21. What is the "dual agency" in real estate?

A. When an agent represents both the buyer and the seller
B. When two agents work for the same client
C. When an agent works for two different real estate firms
D. When an agent sells both commercial and residential properties

Answer: A

Dual agency occurs when a real estate agent represents both the buyer and the seller in the same transaction.

22. What does the Fair Housing Act prohibit?

A. Discrimination based on race, color, religion, sex, or national origin
B. All forms of discrimination
C. Discrimination based on financial status
D. Discrimination based on occupation

Answer: A

The Fair Housing Act prohibits discrimination in housing based on race, color, religion, sex, or national origin.

23. What is earnest money?

A. Money paid by the buyer at the time of the property closing
B. A refundable deposit
C. Money paid by the buyer to show serious intent to purchase
D. Money paid by the seller as a part of the listing agreement

Answer: C

Earnest money is money paid by the buyer to show serious intent to purchase the property.

24. What is a contingency in a real estate contract?

A. A binding clause
B. A non-negotiable term
C. A condition that must be met for the contract to be binding
D. A penalty for breach of contract

Answer: C

A contingency is a condition that must be met for the contract to be binding, such as a home inspection.

25. What is a fiduciary duty?

A. A legal obligation to act in the best interest of another
B. A duty to find the best property for a client
C. A duty to sell a property as quickly as possible
D. A duty to maximize profit

Answer: A

A fiduciary duty is a legal obligation to act in the best interest of another, such as a client.

26. What is a unilateral contract?

A. A contract where only one party makes a promise
B. A contract where both parties make promises
C. A contract that involves more than two parties
D. A contract that is not legally binding

Answer: A

A unilateral contract is a contract where only one party makes a promise, and the other has the option to complete the action.

27. What is the purpose of a disclosure statement?

A. To disclose the agent's commission

B. To disclose any known defects or issues with the property

C. To disclose the buyer's financial status

D. To disclose the terms of the mortgage

Answer: B

The purpose of a disclosure statement is to disclose any known defects or issues with the property to the buyer.

28. What does "time is of the essence" mean in a real estate contract?

A. Deadlines must be strictly adhered to

B. Time limits are flexible

C. The contract has no expiration date

D. The contract can be terminated at any time

Answer: A

"Time is of the essence" means that deadlines set forth in the contract must be strictly adhered to.

29. What is a quitclaim deed?

A. A deed that transfers property with no warranties

B. A deed that includes warranties

C. A deed that transfers leasehold interest

D. A deed that can be easily revoked

Answer: A

A quitclaim deed is a deed that transfers property with no warranties or guarantees.

30. What is the role of a notary public in a real estate transaction?

A. To negotiate the terms
B. To verify the identity of the parties and witness the signing of documents
C. To provide legal advice
D. To inspect the property

Answer: B

The role of a notary public is to verify the identity of the parties and witness the signing of important documents.

31. What is the primary purpose of a title search?

A. To determine the property's market value
B. To verify the legal owner of the property
C. To inspect the condition of the property
D. To assess property taxes

Answer: B

The primary purpose of a title search is to verify the legal owner of the property and ensure there are no liens or other encumbrances.

32. What is a "balloon payment" in a mortgage?

A. A small initial payment
B. A large final payment
C. A regular monthly payment
D. An extra payment to reduce interest

Answer: B

A balloon payment is a large final payment at the end of a loan term, usually after a series of smaller payments.

33. What is the "right of first refusal" in real estate?

A. The right to refuse a sale
B. The right to be the first to purchase a property before the owner sells it to another party
C. The right to refuse to pay rent
D. The right to refuse a home inspection

Answer: B

The right of first refusal allows an individual or entity the opportunity to purchase a property before the owner sells it to another party.

34. What is a "listing agreement"?

A. An agreement between buyer and seller
B. An agreement between a seller and a real estate agent
C. An agreement between a buyer and a real estate agent
D. An agreement between two real estate agents

Answer: B

A listing agreement is a contract between a seller and a real estate agent outlining the terms under which the agent will sell the property.

35. What does "under contract" mean in real estate?

A. The property is being appraised
B. The property is being inspected
C. An offer on the property has been accepted, but the sale is not yet complete
D. The property has been sold

Answer: C

"Under contract" means that an offer on the property has been accepted, but the sale is not yet complete, pending contingencies or other terms.

36. What is the role of a fiduciary in a real estate transaction?

A. To act in the best interest of the client
B. To maximize profits for the brokerage
C. To represent both buyer and seller equally
D. To ensure the property passes inspection

Answer: A

The role of a fiduciary is to act in the best interest of the client, whether that's the buyer or the seller.

37. What does "escrow" refer to in real estate?

A. A type of mortgage loan
B. A neutral third party holding funds or documents until conditions are met
C. A binding contract between buyer and seller
D. A home inspection report

Answer: B

Escrow refers to a neutral third party holding funds or documents until certain conditions are met in a real estate transaction.

38. What is a "contingency" in a real estate contract?

A. A penalty for late payment
B. A condition that must be met for the contract to proceed
C. An optional add-on to the property

D. A mandatory fee paid to the real estate agent

Answer: B

A contingency is a condition that must be met for the contract to proceed, such as a successful home inspection.

⇒ 39. What does "amortization" mean in the context of a mortgage?

A. The process of increasing the loan amount
B. The process of paying off the loan over time
C. The process of adjusting the interest rate
D. The process of transferring the loan to another lender

Answer: B

Amortization is the process of paying off a loan over time through regular payments.

⇒ 40. What is "due diligence" in real estate?

A. The responsibility to investigate a property before purchase
B. The obligation to pay property taxes
C. The requirement to obtain a mortgage pre-approval
D. The duty to disclose all known defects to a buyer

Answer: A

Due diligence is the responsibility of the buyer to investigate a property thoroughly before completing the purchase.

⇒ 41. What is "redlining" in the context of real estate?

A. Drawing property boundaries
B. Discriminatory practice affecting mortgage availability

C. A type of home inspection
D. A negotiation strategy

Answer: B

Redlining is a discriminatory practice where mortgage lenders deny loans or insurance to certain areas based on racial or ethnic composition.

➡ 42. What does "title insurance" protect against?

A. Property damage
B. Mortgage default
C. Legal claims against property ownership
D. Loss of rental income

Answer: C

Title insurance protects against legal claims challenging the ownership of the property.

➡ 43. What is "dual agency" in real estate?

A. When an agent represents both the buyer and the seller
B. When two agents from the same brokerage represent the buyer and the seller
C. When an agent represents two buyers for the same property
D. When an agent represents two sellers for different properties

Answer: A

Dual agency occurs when a real estate agent represents both the buyer and the seller in the same transaction. This can create a conflict of interest and is illegal in some states.

➡ 44. What is a "balloon mortgage"?

A. A mortgage with fluctuating interest rates
B. A mortgage that requires a large final payment

C. A mortgage with no down payment

D. A mortgage paid off in less than 5 years

Answer: B

A balloon mortgage requires a large final payment at the end of the loan term.

45. What is "blockbusting"?

A. Building multiple properties in a short time

B. Encouraging people to sell their homes by instigating fear of a changing neighborhood

C. The process of rezoning land

D. Buying large blocks of property for development

Answer: B

Blockbusting is the practice of encouraging people to sell their homes by instigating fear, often related to racial, ethnic, or social change in a neighborhood.

46. What is a "1031 exchange"?

A. A tax-deferred property exchange

B. A type of mortgage loan

C. A property auction

D. An open house event

Answer: A

A 1031 exchange allows the owner to sell a property and reinvest the proceeds in a new property while deferring capital gains tax.

47. What is "eminent domain"?

A. The right of the government to acquire private property for public use

B. The highest legal ownership of property

C. A type of zoning regulation

D. A clause in a mortgage contract

Answer: A

Eminent domain is the right of the government to acquire private property for public use, usually with compensation.

48. What is "equity" in real estate?

A. The market value of a property

B. The difference between the property's market value and the remaining mortgage balance

C. The initial down payment

D. The annual property tax

Answer: B

Equity is the difference between the market value of the property and the remaining balance on any loans secured by the property.

49. What is "escrow" in a real estate transaction?

A. A legal arrangement where a third party holds funds or documents

B. The initial offer made by a buyer

C. The final stage of mortgage approval

D. A type of home inspection

Answer: A

Escrow is a legal arrangement in which a third party temporarily holds funds or documents until the conditions of a contract are met.

50. What is "net operating income" in real estate investment?

A. Gross income minus operating expenses

B. Gross income plus operating expenses

C. Mortgage payments minus rental income

D. Property value minus mortgage balance

Answer: A

Net operating income is the gross income generated by a property minus the operating expenses, not including mortgage payments or taxes.

Day of the Exam

The day of the Missouri Real Estate License Exam is a pivotal moment in your journey to becoming a licensed real estate agent. This chapter aims to provide you with a comprehensive guide to ensure that you are well-prepared, confident, and equipped to ace the exam.

Pre-Exam Checklist

Documentation

Ensure you have all the required identification documents. Typically, you'll need two forms of ID, one of which must be government-issued and photo-bearing.

Exam Fee

Some testing centers require payment on the day of the exam. Make sure you know the payment methods accepted.

Supplies

Bring at least two pencils, an eraser, and a calculator if allowed. Some centers provide these, but it's better to be prepared.

Dress Code

Dress comfortably but professionally. Layering is a good idea as testing centers can be unpredictably hot or cold.

Nutrition

Eat a balanced meal before heading to the exam center. Avoid too much caffeine, as it can make you jittery.

Arriving at the Testing Center

Timing

Arrive at least 30 minutes early. This gives you time to find parking, go through security, and relax before the exam starts.

Security Measures

Expect to go through a security check. You'll likely be asked to empty your pockets and may be scanned with a metal detector.

Test Room Protocol

Listen carefully to the proctor's instructions. Make sure you understand the rules, as breaking them could result in disqualification.

During the Exam

Time Management

The Missouri Real Estate License Exam is divided into two sections: the national portion and the state-specific portion. Each has its own time limit. Keep an eye on the clock.

Question Strategy

Read each question carefully. Eliminate incorrect answers and make educated guesses if you're unsure.

Taking Breaks

Find out the break policy in advance. Some centers allow breaks, but the clock keeps ticking.

Technical Issues

If you're taking a computer-based test and encounter technical issues, alert the proctor immediately.

Handling Stress and Anxiety

Breathing Techniques

Deep breathing can help calm nerves. Try the 4-7-8 technique: inhale for 4 seconds, hold for 7, and exhale for 8.

Positive Visualization

Imagine a positive outcome to help boost your confidence.

Mini Breaks

If allowed, take short breaks to stretch and refocus.

Special Accommodations

If you have a disability, make sure you've arranged for any necessary accommodations well in advance.

Conclusion

The day of the exam is a culmination of your hard work and preparation. Knowing what to expect and how to navigate the logistics and emotional aspects of the day can make a significant difference in your performance. With the right preparation and mindset, you're well on your way to passing the Missouri Real Estate License Exam and launching a successful career.

After the Exam: Next Steps

Congratulations on completing the Missouri Real Estate License Exam! Whether you've passed or are awaiting results, the journey doesn't end here. This chapter will guide you through the essential steps to take after the exam, from receiving your license to kick-starting your career.

Receiving Your Results

Preliminary Results

If you took a computer-based exam, you'd likely receive preliminary results immediately. However, these are not your official results.

Official Results

Your official results are usually mailed within a few weeks and may also be accessible online. Keep an eye on your mailbox and email.

Failed Attempt

If you didn't pass, don't lose heart. You can retake the exam, but you'll need to wait for the mandatory waiting period to elapse. Use this time to review your weak areas.

Applying for Your License

Application Process

Once you pass the exam, you'll need to apply for your real estate license. This involves submitting an application form, which you can usually find on the Missouri Real Estate Commission's website, along with the required fees.

Background Check

Expect to undergo a background check. Any criminal history could affect your application, so be prepared to provide explanations and documentation if necessary.

Issuance of License

Once your application is approved, you'll receive your license. This is your ticket to practicing real estate in Missouri.

Joining a Brokerage

Research

Start by researching various brokerages to find one that aligns with your career goals. Look for brokerages that offer strong training programs, mentorship, and a good commission structure.

Interviews

You'll need to interview with potential brokerages. Treat this as seriously as a job interview. Come prepared with questions and be ready to discuss your long-term career plans.

Contract and Onboarding

Once you've chosen a brokerage, you'll sign a contract and go through an onboarding process, which usually includes training and introduction to the brokerage's tools and systems.

Building Your Business

Marketing

Start building your brand. This could mean setting up a professional website, creating business cards, or even launching a social media marketing campaign.

Networking

Networking is crucial in real estate. Attend industry events, join real estate associations, and don't underestimate the power of a good referral.

Client Management

You'll need a system to manage your clients. Many agents use Customer Relationship Management (CRM) software for this purpose.

Continuing Education

Mandatory Courses

Missouri requires real estate agents to complete continuing education courses to renew their license. Make sure you're aware of these requirements and complete them on time.

Optional Courses

There are also optional courses you can take to specialize in certain areas, like commercial real estate or property management.

Financial Planning

Taxes

As a real estate agent, you're essentially a small business owner. This means you'll need to manage your taxes, which may include quarterly estimated payments.

Retirement

Don't forget about retirement. Consider setting up a retirement account specifically for self-employed individuals.

Ethics and Legal Considerations

Code of Ethics

Many real estate agents choose to join associations that have a Code of Ethics, which you're expected to uphold.

Legal Updates

Laws and regulations change. Stay updated to ensure you're always in compliance.

Career Growth

Mentorship

Consider finding a mentor to guide you through the early stages of your career.

Scaling Your Business

As your business grows, you may need to hire an assistant or even a team of agents to work under you.

Diversification

Think about diversifying your income streams. This could mean getting into property management or even real estate investment.

Conclusion

The period following your exam is crucial for setting the stage for a successful career. From receiving your license to joining a brokerage and building your business, each step is an opportunity to establish yourself in the industry. With careful planning, continuous learning, and a commitment to ethical practice, you can look forward to a rewarding career in Missouri's real estate market.

Career Development

Congratulations on passing the Missouri Real Estate License Exam and taking the first steps into your real estate career! But what comes next? This chapter aims to provide a comprehensive guide on career development for new real estate agents. From setting goals to leveraging technology, we'll cover all the facets that contribute to a successful career in real estate.

Setting Career Goals

Short-Term Goals

Your first year in real estate will be a whirlwind of learning and growing. Short-term goals could include completing your first sale, joining a reputable brokerage, or even just mastering the local market.

Long-Term Goals

Long-term goals could range from becoming a top-selling agent in your area to owning your own brokerage. These goals will guide your career path and help you make important decisions along the way.

SMART Goals

When setting goals, make sure they are Specific, Measurable, Achievable, Relevant, and Time-bound (SMART). This framework ensures that your goals are well-defined and attainable.

Building a Personal Brand

Importance

In real estate, your personal brand is your business. It's how clients perceive you and why they'll choose you over competitors.

Steps to Build a Brand

1. Identify Your Unique Selling Proposition (USP): What sets you apart from other agents?
2. Create a Professional Image: This includes professional attire, business cards, and a well-designed website.
3. Social Media Presence: Use platforms like Facebook, Instagram, and LinkedIn to reach a broader audience.

Networking

Industry Events

Attend industry events, seminars, and workshops. These are excellent opportunities to meet other professionals and potential clients.

Real Estate Associations

Joining a real estate association can provide you with valuable resources and a network of like-minded professionals.

Referrals

Never underestimate the power of a good referral. Satisfied clients are your best advocates.

Leveraging Technology

MLS Systems

The Multiple Listing Service (MLS) is an essential tool for any real estate agent. It provides up-to-date information on properties and is a valuable resource for both buying and selling.

CRM Software

Customer Relationship Management (CRM) software helps you manage your clients, keep track of interactions, and schedule follow-ups.

Virtual Tours

In today's digital age, offering virtual tours can give you an edge. It allows potential buyers to view properties without having to be physically present.

Time Management

Prioritization

Learn to prioritize your tasks. Not everything that is urgent is important.

Scheduling

Use tools like Google Calendar to schedule your day. Allocate specific time slots for different activities, including personal time.

Work-Life Balance

Maintaining a work-life balance is crucial for long-term success. Burnout is a real concern in high-stress professions like real estate.

Financial Planning

Budgeting

Create a budget to track your income and expenses. This will give you a clear picture of your financial health.

Taxes

As an independent contractor, you're responsible for your own taxes. Consider hiring an accountant who specializes in real estate.

Retirement Planning

Start planning for retirement early. Look into Individual Retirement Accounts (IRAs) specifically designed for self-employed individuals.

Continuing Education

Mandatory Courses

Most states require real estate agents to complete a certain number of continuing education hours to renew their license.

Specializations

Consider specializing in a particular type of real estate, such as commercial properties or luxury homes, to set yourself apart.

Mentorship and Coaching

Finding a Mentor

A mentor can provide invaluable insights and guidance. Look for someone who has experience in the real estate market you're interested in.

Coaching Programs

There are various coaching programs designed specifically for real estate agents. These programs can provide you with the skills and knowledge to advance your career.

Scaling Your Business

Hiring an Assistant

As your business grows, administrative tasks can take up a significant amount of your time. Hiring an assistant can free you up to focus on revenue-generating activities.

Forming a Team

If you're handling a large volume of transactions, it might be beneficial to form a team. A team can provide specialized skills and help manage a larger client base.

Conclusion

Career development in real estate is a continuous process that requires strategic planning, ongoing education, and adaptability. By setting clear goals, building a strong personal brand, and leveraging the latest technology, you can set yourself up for a long and successful career. Remember, the sky's the limit, so aim high and don't stop until you get there.

Conclusion

As we reach the conclusion of this comprehensive guide, " Missouri Real Estate License Exam: Best Test Prep Book to Help You Get Your License!", I want to extend my heartfelt congratulations to you. The journey to becoming a licensed real estate agent is a challenging one, filled with its share of trials and tribulations. But remember, the journey of a thousand miles begins with a single step, and you've already taken several by investing your time and energy into this book.

The Road Ahead

We've covered a lot of ground together, from understanding the intricacies of the Missouri real estate market to the nitty-gritty details of the application process, exam format, and even career development. But this book is not an end; it's a beginning. The real estate industry is ever-changing, and continuous learning is the key to staying ahead. Make it a point to keep up with industry trends, legal changes, and market dynamics.

The Importance of Networking and Mentorship

One of the most valuable lessons you'll learn in your career is that real estate is a people business. The relationships you build today could be your biggest assets tomorrow. Whether it's through networking events, social media, or mentorship—never underestimate the power of a strong professional network.

The Role of Technology

In today's digital age, leveraging technology is not just an option; it's a necessity. From CRM systems to virtual tours, technology can give you an edge in a highly competitive market. Make sure you're not left behind.

Ethics and Legal Considerations

As we discussed in the chapter on Ethics and Legal Considerations, maintaining high ethical standards is crucial for long-term success. Your reputation is your most valuable asset, and once tarnished, it's challenging to rebuild. Always adhere to the legal guidelines and ethical norms of the industry.

The Power of Resilience

You'll face setbacks, like failing deals or tough clients, but remember that resilience is your greatest ally. The most successful real estate agents are not those who never fail, but those who never quit.

Your Next Steps

As you close this book, you're not just ending a chapter but opening a new one in your real estate career. Your next steps are crucial. Whether it's preparing for the exam or planning your first property showing, move forward with confidence and conviction.

Final Words

Thank you for allowing this book to be a part of your real estate journey. It's been a pleasure to provide you with the tools and knowledge to help you succeed. I wish you all the best in your endeavors, and may your career in real estate be fulfilling and prosperous.

Here's to your success and to a bright future in the Missouri real estate market!

Made in the USA
Monee, IL
04 May 2025